Peter Lucantoni with Brian Dyer

Cambridge IGCSE®
English as a Second Language

Exam Preparation Guide

Reading and Writing

Completely Cambridge – Cambridge resources for Cambridge qualifications

Cambridge University Press works closely with University of Cambridge International Examinations (CIE) as parts of the University of Cambridge. We enable thousands of students to pass their CIE exams by providing comprehensive, high-quality, endorsed resources.

To find out more about University of Cambridge International Examinations visit www.cie.org.uk

To find out more about Cambridge University Press visit www.cambridge.org/cie

CAMBRIDGE UNIVERSITY PRESS
Cambridge, New York, Melbourne, Madrid, Cape Town,
Singapore, São Paulo, Delhi, Mexico City

Cambridge University Press
The Edinburgh Building, Cambridge CB2 8RU, UK

www.cambridge.org
Information on this title: www.cambridge.org/9780521151344

First published 2011
Reprinted 2012

Printed in the United Kingdom at the University Press, Cambridge

A catalogue record for this publication is available from the British Library

ISBN 978-0-521-15134-4 Paperback

® IGCSE is the registered trademark of University of Cambridge International Examinations.

Contents

Acknowledgements

The author and publishers are grateful for the permissions granted to reproduce materials in either the original or adapted form. While every effort has been made, it has not always been possible to identify the sources of all the materials used, or to trace all copyright holders. If any omissions are brought to our notice, we will be happy to include the appropriate acknowledgements on reprinting.

Texts

Examination questions throughout reproduced by permission of the University of Cambridge Local Examinations Syndicate

p. 30 © www.snowdonia-active.com; p. 32 Monkey World, www.monkeyworld. org; p. 34 adapted from Boots information leaflet 'Your guide to managing hayfever', 2007; p. 36 Stephanie Peatling / National Geographic Stock, article republished in *The Week*, Oman; p. 38 adapted from part of article from the *Oman Daily Observer*, April 2008; p. 40 used by permission of Nathan Morley, *Cyprus Mail*; p. 74 used by permission of the *Yemen Observer*; p. 76 adapted from 'Cairo's new cabs' by Adam Morrow in *Gulf Life*, Ink Publishing; p. 78 adapted from 'In parkour, the city is gym' by Dorene Internicola, Reuters, October 2005, republished in *Arab News*, Saudi, all rights reserved, republication or redistribution of Thomson Reuters content, including by framing or similar means, is expressly prohibited without prior written consent of Thomson Reuters – Thomson Reuters and its logo are registered trademarks or trademarks of the Thomson Reuters group of companies around the world, © Thomson Reuters 2009, Thomson Reuters journalists are subject to an Editorial Handbook which requires fair representation and disclosure of relevant interests; p. 80 reproduced by kind permissions of Sainsbury's Supermarkets Ltd; p. 100 adapted from Le Meridian hotel in-room magazine; p. 102 adapted from 'Mission Accomplished' in *The Week*, pages 1–4, 13 May 2009, published by Apex Press and Publishing, Sultanate of Oman, www.theweek.co.om; p. 104 adapted from 'Be calm for your exams' by The Hindu, *The Gulf Today*, February 2008

Photographs

Cover image © ImageState / Alamy; p. 3 © Daniel H. Bailey / Corbis; p. 32 © Corbis / SuperStock; p. 34 © Michael Keller / CORBIS; p. 40 used by permission of Nathan Morley, Cyprus Mail; p. 56 BlendImages / SuperStock; p. 58 © Brad Walker / SuperStock; p. 60 © Walter Geiersperger / Corbis; p. 65 © Moodboard / SuperStock; p. 76 used with permission of Victoria Hazou; p. 78 Cusp / SuperStock; p. 100 © Robert Harding Picture Library / SuperStock; p. 104 © Frederick Bass / fstop / Corbis; p. 120 Brownstock Inc. / Alamy

Introduction

This *IGCSE English as a Second Language Exam Preparation Guide* provides extra guidance and practice in each of the seven examination exercises for both Core and Extended students in Papers 1 and 2 (Reading and Writing). While most of you will be using the corresponding IGCSE English as a Second Language Coursebook 2 and Workbook 2, this Exam Preparation Guide can also be used independently, or alongside other IGCSE English as a Second Language coursebooks.

The guide is divided into five units, with each one focusing on one or more different exam exercises. The units all follow a similar pattern: **A** Introduction, **B** Preparation, **C** Exam focus and **D** Exam practice. In Section **A** (Introduction) you will find clear information about what the exercises look like, what you need to be aware of, and what the examiners are looking for in your answers; in Section **B** (Preparation) you will find guidance about how to answer the questions; in Section **C** (Exam focus) you will have the chance to read and comment on exam answers from students, and see what the examiners said about their answers; and in Section **D** (Exam practice) there are lots of exam-type questions for you to practise.

You do not need to start at the beginning of the Guide and work through to the end – you can choose to start at any point. For example, if you need to practise Exercise 5 (the summary) you can go straight to the unit on Exercise 5, or if you want some help with Exercises 1 and 2 (reading comprehension), you should start with that unit, and so on. Check the Contents page to find your way around the Guide.

We hope you enjoy using this Exam Preparation Guide, and we wish you success in your IGCSE E2L exams!

Peter Lucantoni and Brian Dyer

Exercises 1 and 2

In this unit you will learn about Exercises 1 and 2, the two reading comprehension exercises in the IGCSE E2L examination, and practise the skills you need.

A Introduction

What are Exercises 1 and 2?

Exercises 1 and 2 in both the Core and Extended papers assess reading comprehension. You need to read a text and answer questions which test your reading comprehension from **skimming** and reading for **gist** (understanding the main ideas) in Exercise 1 and more detailed understanding from **scanning** in Exercise 2.

You will see the text on the left-hand page, and the questions and answer lines on the opposite page. The number of marks available for each question is given at the end of the answer line. Exercise 2 includes a diagram or chart which will contain the answer to one of the questions.

Exercise 1

Read the following information about the sport of orienteering, and then answer the questions on the opposite page.

Orienteering – the path to adventure and fun

Orienteering developed in the 1930s in Sweden. It is a mixture of cross-country running and map reading in order to complete a fixed course in the quickest possible time. It spread slowly through Europe in the middle of the 1960s, and it was not until after the 1976 World Championships in Scotland that more and more people really began to enjoy it.

Different levels of activity

Orienteering is the ideal adventure sport for outdoor enthusiasts of all ages and abilities – both individuals and family groups. There is a variety of levels, with children as young as seven starting on simple string courses, where coloured tapes show the way. There is a range of courses, usually graduated using colour codes based on length and difficulty. For example, a beginner's yellow course is fairly straightforward and around two kilometres long. The brown course is usually the most difficult and the longest course at eight kilometres or more.

(a) Where did orienteering originate?

_____ [1]

(b) When did orienteering suddenly become popular in Europe?

_____ [1]

(c) What helps to make the course easier for young children?

_____ [1]

(d) What are the **two** reasons for colour-coding the courses?

_____

_____ [1]

Source: Cambridge IGCSE E2L (0510/12) May/June 2008, pages 2–3, Exercise 1

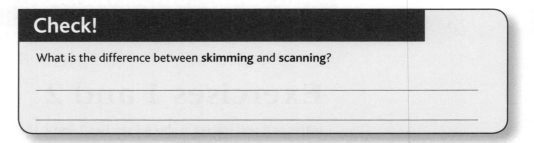

Check!

What is the difference between **skimming** and **scanning**?

_____

_____

How many marks are there?

Exercise 1

In the Core paper there are six marks in total, while in the Extended paper there are eight. Sometimes you may need to find two or more pieces of information in order to get one mark; at other times one question may be worth two marks.

Exercise 2

In the Core paper there are 10 marks available, while in the Extended paper there are 14. Sometimes you may need to find two or more pieces of information in order to get one mark; at other times one question may be worth two marks. The final question in the Extended paper is always worth four marks, where you need to give four pieces of information.

What's the difference between the Core and Extended papers?

Both the Core and Extended papers require you to apply skimming and scanning skills. However, in the final question in the Extended paper you need to write a more detailed answer containing enough information for a maximum of four marks.

What are the assessment objectives?

In Exercise 1 for both the Core and Extended papers there is only one Reading assessment objective:

- understand and respond to information presented in a variety of forms (Reading assessment objective 1).

In Exercise 2 the same assessment objective applies; however, there is an extra Reading assessment objective for the Extended paper:

- infer information from texts (R4).

Check!

What do you think _**infer**_ means? Write your answer and then check in a dictionary.

_____

_____

What do Exercises 1 and 2 look like?

In both the Core and Extended papers, the texts you need to read are on the left-hand page and the questions are opposite. You do not need to turn a page in order to find the questions or where to write your answers. The text for Exercise 1 will be taken from an advertisement, brochure, leaflet, guide, report or manual, and will often have headings and sub-headings. The Exercise 2 text is usually a report or newspaper or magazine article, and it will include a graph, chart or some other visual.

What do I have to do?

Exercise 1

In Exercise 1 (Core and Extended) you need to write short answers – this will often be a single word or phrase, as longer answers are **not** needed. It is important to look at the text heading and any subheadings first to get an idea of the topic, and then to read the questions carefully. As you read the questions, identify and underline the key word or words in each one. Remember that key words will show you in which part of the text the answer is likely to be; and remember that words in the text may appear differently in the questions: this is called **paraphrasing**. Also think about the type of answer that is required: a number, a quantity, a place, a name, a reason, and so on. Finally, remember that you should simply find and copy the answer using the words from the text wherever possible – there is no need to change anything.

Remember!

- Write short answers for Exercise 1 – maybe a single word.
- Look at headings and subheadings to get an idea about the text.
- Read questions carefully – identify and underline key words in each question.
- Key words will show you where to look in the text for your answers.
- Words in the text may be different from in the questions.
- Just find and copy the answers – no need to change anything.

Look at this example:

Orienteering – the path to adventure and fun

Orienteering developed in the 1930s in Sweden. It is a mixture of cross-country running and map reading in order to complete a fixed course in the quickest possible time. It spread slowly through Europe in the middle of the 1960s, and it was not until after the 1976 World Championships in Scotland that more and more people really began to enjoy it.

Source: Cambridge IGCSE E2L (0510/11) May/June 2008, page 2, Exercise 1

Now look at the first two questions:

(a) Where did orienteering originate?

(b) When did orienteering suddenly become popular in Europe?

The key words in **(a)** are *Where* and *originate*. In the text, *originate* does not appear, but the word *developed* leads you to the answer. This question asks you *Where?* so the answer must be a place: *Sweden*.

In **(b)** the key words are *When* and *popular*. Once again, the key words do not appear in the text, but *popular* leads to *enjoy* and therefore to the answer to the question *When?* So the answer must therefore be a time: *after the 1976 World Championships (in Scotland)*.

Exercise 2

In Exercise 2 you may need to write longer answers as more detailed information is often needed. However, you should still keep your answers short and a complete sentence is usually not necessary. By writing too much the actual answer may get lost! Don't forget that some questions need two pieces of information for one mark, while other questions may give two marks.

Remember!

- You may need to write longer answers in Exercise 2.
- Complete sentences are not always necessary.
- Some questions need **two** pieces of information for **one** mark.

Look at these examples:

What negative ideas do people often have about the world underground? Give **two** details.

_____ [1]

Source: Cambridge IGCSE E2L (0510/12) May/June 2008, page 5, Exercise 2

How have visitors damaged the walls of the cave? Give **two** details.

(i) _____ [1]

(ii) _____ [1]

Source: Cambridge IGCSE E2L (0510/22) May/June 2008, page 5, Exercise 2

What do I need to know?

There are no half marks! If the question is worth one mark and asks you for two details, you must supply both pieces of information to get the mark. If you only supply one detail instead of two, you get 0 not ½.

In the final question of Exercise 2 in the Extended paper there are always four marks available. These marks are awarded for four pieces of information from the text, usually around the same theme.

Look at this example:

> Apart from damaging the interior of the cave, how has the area changed as a result of tourism? Give **four** details.
>
> _____
>
> _____
>
> _____
>
> _____ [4]
>
> Source: Cambridge IGCSE E2L (0510/22) May/June 2008, page 5, Exercise 2

You do **not** need to write a paragraph for this question – simply give four pieces of information in note form.

Remember!

- Questions are usually in the same order as the information in the text.
- In the final question of the Extended paper the information can be from anywhere in the text. Give your answers in note form **not** a paragraph.

B Preparation

EXERCISE 1 – EXTENDED

Activity 1

You are going to look at an exercise from an IGCSE examination paper. Before you read the Exercise 1 on page **6**, answer these three questions:

a What do you know about the content of the text **before** you read it?

_____

_____

b Does the layout of the text help you in any way? How?

_____

_____

c Think of **two** things that you might read about in the four main sections: *Where?, The experience, The environment* and *Safari options*.

_____

_____

_____

_____

Exercise 1

Read the following information about whale safaris, and then answer the questions on the opposite page.

Whale wildlife safari

Where?

Our destination is the coastal inlets in the far north of Norway. There is one special deep water area where every year, around October time, large numbers of orca whales can be found. They are visible from the main ship but if you want to see the whales at close quarters, you can either get into a small inflatable raft or even swim with the creatures.

The experience

In one of the most fantastic experiences you will ever have, you become part of the arctic wildlife. Once inside the Arctic circle you see the whales, up to 700 of them, following the vast quantities of herring fish shoals which they love to feed on. You can see the White-Tailed Sea Eagles which also feed on fish shoals with the whales. In addition, the scientists and students working on different aspects of the orca whale's behaviour give workshops and lectures on board ship.

The environment

In October the days are short and the nights long, dark and cold, but these can be spectacular since the Northern Lights, also known as the Aurora Borealis, literally light up the night sky with their fantastic colours. The whole area has wild and beautiful scenery including huge and majestic mountains where eagles rest before swooping down to eat the fish below them in the lakes.

Safari options

Basic safari

This includes your flight to Norway and a trip on a large whale-watching boat in a group of up to 90 people. Often the curiosity of the whales brings them to the surface and close to the boat where you may see whole families of whales. This is a five to six hour safari. A light lunch is served on board.

Zodiac safari

Here you get a closer view of the whales on a smaller boat. The boats are among the safest in the world so there is no need to worry even though you get very close to the water. You have three wonderful hours of whale watching, almost at the same level as the whales themselves. Children must be at least ten years old and accompanied by an adult.

Snorkelling safari

This is only for the most adventurous and only available if weather conditions are suitable. You are equipped with a warm waterproof suit so that you can swim and meet the whales in their own environment, the sea! You have to be 16 years or older for this adventure.

Source: Cambridge IGCSE E2L (0510/22) May/June 2008, page 2, Exercise 1

Activity 2

Quickly skim the questions below and then read the text more carefully.
Check if the things you thought about in Activity **1c** are included.

Activity 3

Now read the questions carefully for the *Whale wildlife safari* text.

(a) At what time of year can the whales be seen?

_____ [1]

(b) What other kinds of wildlife apart from whales will you be able to see?
Give **two** details.

_____

_____ [1]

(c) How can you get more information about the whales?

_____ [1]

(d) What is sometimes special about nights in the Arctic?

_____ [1]

(e) On the Basic safari:

   (i) what brings whales to the surface?

_____ [1]

   (ii) what might tourists see?

_____ [1]

(f) On the Zodiac safari, what restrictions are there for children? Give
two details.

_____

_____ [1]

(g) In what way is the Snorkelling safari only for the adventurous?

_____ [1]

[Total: 8]

Source: Cambridge IGCSE E2L (0510/22) May/June 2008, page 3, Exercise 1

Activity 4

What do you notice about the marks available for questions **(b)**, **(e)** and **(f)**?

_____

_____

What do you need to be careful about?

_____

_____

Activity 5

Read the questions again in more detail and underline the key words or phrases in each one.

Example:

(a) At what <u>time of year</u> can the <u>whales be seen</u>?

Activity 6

Think about the words and phrases you have underlined. What type of information do you need to look for in the text?

Example:

time of year – perhaps a season or a month

whales be seen – perhaps 'appear', 'visible'

_____

_____

Activity 7

Without looking at the text, in which of the four main sections do you think you will find the answers to the first four questions, **(a)–(d)**? Why? Can you always decide? Complete as much of the table as you can.

Question	Section	Reason
(a)	Where?	because the question asks 'when' (at what time of year) – probably in same place in text as it gives information about 'where'
(b)		
(c)		
(d)		

Activity 8

Look at the _Safari options_ section again: how many paragraphs are there?

_____

Activity 9

Now look at questions **(e)–(g)**: where in the text will you find the answers to these questions?

_____

_____

Activity 10

Here are all the answers to questions **(a)–(g)** but they have been mixed up. Match the answers with the questions.

1   you meet the whales in their own environment / you swim with the whales _____

2   **(i)** curiosity / whale-watching boat **(ii)** whole families of whales _____

3   Aurora Borealis / the Northern Lights / lights in the sky _____

4   herring/fish **and** (white-tailed sea) eagles (**both needed**) _____

5   (around) October (time) _____

6   they must be at least 10 (years old) **and** accompanied by an adult (**both needed**) _____

7   workshops/lectures _____

EXERCISE 1 – CORE

Activity 11

You are going to look at an exercise from an IGCSE examination paper. Before you read the Exercise 1 on page **10**, answer these three questions:

a   What do you know about the content of the text **before** you read it?

_____

_____

b   Does the layout of the text help you in any way? How?

_____

_____

c   Think of **two** things that you might read about in the three main sections: *Train from London to Europe by Eurostar*, *Somewhere magical* and *Easy to book, easy to travel*.

_____

_____

_____

Exercise 1

Read the following article about travel from London to Paris, and then answer the questions on the opposite page.

Train from London to Europe by Eurostar

With Eurostar, Paris is only three hours from London. It used to take three journeys – a trip to the airport, a flight, and then a third journey from airport to city centre. With Eurostar, it's one journey direct from city centre to city centre. It is one of the most technologically advanced trains in the world, speeding you effortlessly at 290 km per hour through the beautiful countryside of Europe. And on Eurostar not only do you save time, but your time belongs to you. You have space. You can read, relax and even enjoy a delicious meal.

Somewhere magical

Eurostar can carry you straight to the centre of Disneyland in Paris. During the school holidays and from April to September, the direct service operates daily. At other times of the year, it runs at weekends. You can spend your journey planning the fun, and, with over 50 attractions for both adults and children at the Disneyland Park, there is plenty of fun to choose from. It's a wonderful place where everybody is guaranteed an unforgettable experience.

Easy to book, easy to travel

Our friendly, multilingual staff are available at all times to help you, both at the terminal and on the train. To reserve your ticket, the telephone booking line is open from 08:00 to 21:00 Monday to Saturday and 09:00 to 17:00 on Sundays, or visit the website at www.eurostar.com where you will find some great ideas and useful information about destinations to help you plan your trip.

Eurostar tickets can be booked up to 90 days in advance. Whether you have booked on the telephone or the internet, we can send the tickets to your home address, or, for last-minute bookings, you can collect them at the Eurostar station just before your journey.

Source: Cambridge IGCSE E2L (0510/01) May/June 2007, page 2, Exercise 1

Activity 12

Quickly skim the questions below and then read the text more carefully. Check if the things you thought about in Activity **11c** are included.

Activity 13

Now read the questions for the *Train from London* text.

(a) How fast can the Eurostar train travel?

_____ [1]

(b) Apart from relaxing, what else can you do on the train? Give **two** details.

(i) _____

(ii) _____ [1]

(c) How often does the train travel to Disneyland in July?

_____ [1]

(d) What does Disneyland offer for all the family?

_____ [1]

(e) How can Eurostar staff help if you do not speak English?

_____ [1]

(f) Give **two** ways of booking a ticket.

(i) _____

(ii) _____ [1]

[Total: 6]

Source: Cambridge IGCSE E2L (0510/01) May/June 2007, page 3, Exercise 1

Activity 14

What do you notice about the marks available for questions **(b)** and **(f)**? What do you need to be careful about?

_____

_____

Activity 15

Read the questions again in more detail and underline the key words or phrases in each one.

Example:

(a) How <u>fast</u> can the Eurostar train travel?

Activity 16

Think about the words and phrases you have underlined. What type of information do you need to look for in the text?

Example:

fast – speed, kph, kilometres

_____

_____

Activity 17

Without looking at the text, in which of the three main sections do you think you will find the answers to questions **(a)–(f)**? Why? Can you always decide? Complete as much of the table as you can.

Question	Section	Reason
(a)	Train from London to Europe by Eurostar	because the question does not really match the other two paragraphs; also, first question, first paragraph
(b)		
(c)		
(d)		
(e)		
(f)		

Activity 18

Here are all the answers to questions **(a)–(f)** but they have been mixed up. Match the answers with the questions.

1   by phone **and** on the internet/website/www.eurostar.com (**both needed**) _____

2   daily _____

3   read **and** enjoy a meal (**both needed**) _____

4   they are multilingual / they can speak other languages _____

5   290 km per hour _____

6   many (50) attractions (for both adults and children) / an unforgettable experience / plenty of fun _____

EXERCISE 2 – CORE AND EXTENDED

You are going to look at an exercise from an IGCSE examination paper.

Activity 19

Before you read the Exercise 2 on page **14**, answer these two questions:

a How does the layout and design of the text differ from the two Exercise 1 texts you read on pages **6** and **10**?

_____

_____

b What does this Exercise 2 text include which the others did not?

_____

_____

Activity 20

Read the questions for the text on page **15**.

Note that questions **(a)–(g)** are the same for both the Core and Extended papers. Question **(h)** is for the Extended paper only.

Activity 21

What do you notice about the marks available for questions **(a)**, **(c)**, **(d)**, **(f)** and **(h)**? What do you need to be careful about?

_____

_____

Activity 22

Read the questions again in more detail and underline the key words or phrases in each one.

Example:

(a) What <u>negative ideas</u> do people often have about the world underground?
Give **two details**.

Activity 23

Think about the words and phrases you have underlined. What type of information do you need to look for in the text?

Example:

negative ideas – something unpleasant, perhaps something scary or frightening, bats, rats ...

two details

_____

_____

Exercise 2

Read the article below about an amazing underground cave, and then answer the questions below.

A visit to the underworld

(1) When professional photographer Kusmatiya Sharakya descended into the underground world of the Goa Cerme cave near Yogyakarta in Indonesia, he encountered a beautiful subterranean environment. Here he describes his visit:

(2) 'People often imagine that the world beneath the earth is scary and in total darkness, but this is not always true. The Goa Cerme cave has a spectacular beauty and many unusual features.

(3) 'Our group entered the cave and our fears disappeared immediately when the lights from our lanterns revealed the interior filled with a huge variety of incredible forms and shapes. We listened to the soft sound of water slowly running at the bottom of the cave, the echo of water droplets and the gusts of wind rushing from the cave entrance. They all encouraged us to venture deeper and explore the secrets of this mysterious underworld.

(4) 'We walked through the knee-deep water of a small river at the bottom of the cave, sometimes jumping from stone to stone, admiring a new and amazing sight at every corner. The tunnels were very narrow in places and we always had to keep a look-out for sharp stone formations hanging low from the ceiling which could have easily hurt our heads.

(5) 'Under the guidance of the Department of Geology at the local university, we proceeded deep into the cave and took photographs of every attractive sight. The Department also provided us with caving equipment such as head lamps, rubber boots, safety helmets and ropes.

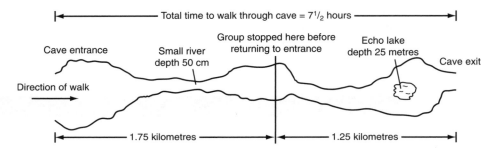

(6) 'We could hardly believe that four and a half hours had passed since we entered the cave. Unfortunately there was not enough time to explore the remainder of the cave up to the exit, which, according to our guides, would have taken another three hours of gentle walking.

(7) 'This three-kilometre long Goa Cerme cave is located to the south of Yogyakarta. The local people know it as a tranquil place to seek divine guidance. However, the area has lately become popular as a tourist destination and commercial buildings and food stalls have started to appear. The quiet atmosphere has gradually disappeared. The entrance to the cave now has concrete walkways which destroy the natural and unspoiled appearance of the place.

(8) 'In addition, the great numbers of people going through the cave have caused some damage to the inside – like the black soot from the visitors' oil lamps that now covers much of the cave's walls and ceiling. Undisciplined tourists have left their rubbish behind and removed stones from the walls of the cave as souvenirs. Hopefully these bad habits will disappear soon so that we can all enjoy the rare beauty of this natural wonder for many years to come.'

Source: Cambridge IGCSE E2L (0510/21) May/June 2008, page 4, Exercise 2

(a) What negative ideas do people often have about the world underground? Give **two** details.

_____ [1]

(b) What did the lanterns show the photographers?

_____ [1]

(c) What were the obstacles that members of the group encountered:

(i) above them? _____ [1]

(ii) below them? _____ [1]

(d) In what ways did the local university help the photographers? Give **two** details.

(i) _____ [1]

(ii) _____ [1]

(e) According to the diagram, how far was the group from the exit when it stopped?

_____ [1]

(f) How have visitors damaged the walls of the cave? Give **two** details.

(i) _____ [1]

(ii) _____ [1]

(g) What is the photographer's main hope for the future of the caves?

_____ [1]

(h) Apart from damaging the interior of the cave, how has the area changed as a result of tourism? Give **four** details.

_____

_____

_____

_____ [4]

[Total: 14]

Source: Cambridge IGCSE E2L (0510/21) May/June 2008, page 5, Exercise 2

Activity 24

Read the second paragraph of the text on page **14**. Which of the following is the best answer to question **(a)**. Why?

1 scary and dark

2 Kusmatiya Sharakya says that people imagine that the world beneath the earth is scary and in total darkness

3 the world beneath the earth is scary and in total darkness

4 the world underground is scary

5 the negative ideas are scary and darkness

_____

_____

Activity 25

Look at question **(b)** on page **15** and paragraph 3 of the text. What does the word _lanterns_ mean? Try to guess from the context. Do you need to fully understand the word to answer the question correctly?

_____

_____

Activity 26

Look at question **(c)** on page **15**. What does the word _obstacles_ mean? This is an important word because it leads you directly to the answers in paragraph 4 (remember that there are **two** marks).

_____

_____

Activity 27

The key words in question **(d)** are _local university_ and _help_. These words should take you directly to paragraph 5 where you will see _the Department of Geology at the local university_. Notice that the second sentence begins: _The Department also provided ..._ Now answer question **(d)**.

_____

_____

Activity 28

Question **(e)** says _According to the diagram,_ so the answer to this question is not written in the text itself. The key words in the question are _stopped_ and _exit_ and both these words appear in the diagram. Now answer question **(e)**.

_____

_____

Activity 29

Look carefully at question **(f)**. This question requires you to find two ways in which visitors have damaged the walls of the cave – the keys words are *damaged* and *visitors*. Read the final paragraph – there are three points here about what visitors have done, but only **two** of them mention the cave's walls. Which two?

_____

_____

Activity 30

Question **(g)** might be tricky because you may have forgotten that the text is the voice of the photographer mentioned in the first paragraph! Answer the question.

_____

_____

Activity 31

The final question **(h)** only appears in the Extended paper. The words *Apart from … the cave* tell you to look for other changes in the area which have been caused by visitors and tourists. You should not repeat anything you have already written in answers to other questions, such as question **(f)**. Write your answer to question **(h)**.

_____

_____

C Exam focus

EXERCISE 1

You are going to look at some sample answers from IGCSE students to the Core and Extended Exercise 1 question on page **18**.

Activity 32

Before you read the sample answers and the text in detail, look at the main title, *Fantastic leaves*, and the five subheadings. What do you think you might read about in each one?

_____

_____

_____

_____

_____

Exercise 1

Read the following article about banana leaves, and then answer the questions on the opposite page.

Fantastic leaves

We all know about bananas. They are rich in vitamins A, B6 and C and in potassium, and humans eat large numbers of them. Only rice, wheat and maize are consumed in greater quantities. Bananas are grown in about 130 countries, which is more than any other fruit crop.

But what about the banana leaf itself? It is valued in many parts of the world for its beauty and fragrance and it has many additional uses.

Eating naturally

The banana leaf may have been the original equivalent of the modern paper plate. Eating food served on a banana leaf is more hygienic than eating food off plastic, steel or ceramic plates. Also, when the meal is finished, the leaf can be disposed of in an environmentally friendly way.

Non-stick

A banana leaf can also serve as a non-stick frying pan. This means that you don't have to use oil and it is a healthy way of cooking food. The many uses of banana leaves make them a vital part of traditional life in countries such as Sri Lanka and they are a perfect example of the human ability to find a purpose for even the most ordinary items. When banana leaves are used to wrap packets of rice and curry, they add a distinct flavour to the food.

And when it rains ...

On rainy days, villagers in many parts of the world hold banana leaves over their heads to keep them from getting wet! In addition, not only people but also plants such as cocoa, coffee and black pepper benefit from the leaf as a means of shade.

Get packing

In Sri Lanka, when delicate fruits are being transported by lorry, banana leaves serve as packing materials to prevent them from getting squashed. In this way they are far more eco-friendly than plastic wrapping material. Another benefit is that when banana leaves are used, they help to retain the freshness of the fruits.

Decorative uses

Banana leaves are sometimes used as wedding decorations, where they are thought to bring good luck and prosperity to the couple getting married. In places such as Haiti, when the leaves are dried, they are woven to make attractive hampers and salad bowls.

The banana and its leaf together form one of nature's truly versatile creations.

Source: Cambridge IGCSE E2L (0510/11) May/June 2009, page 2, Exercise 1

Activity 33

Now look at the Core questions **(a)–(f)** below and the Extended questions **(a)–(g)** on page **20**. Which questions require more than one piece of information in your answer? How many marks are available for these questions? Which Extended question does not appear in the Core paper?

_____

_____

_____

CORE

(a) Which three foods do people eat most in the world?

_____ [1]

(b) Which ingredient is not required if you use banana leaves when frying food?

_____ [1]

(c) What is one benefit of wrapping rice and curry in banana leaves?

_____ [1]

(d) How do the leaves help other crops when they are growing?

_____ [1]

(e) What are the advantages of using banana leaves as packaging? Give **two** details.

_____ [1]

(f) Why are banana leaves popular as wedding decorations?

_____ [1]

[Total: 6]

Source: Cambridge IGCSE E2L (0510/11) May/June 2009, page 3, Exercise 1

EXTENDED

(a) Which three foods do people eat most in the world?

_____ [1]

(b) What advantages are there in using banana leaves instead of plates?

(i) _____ [1]

(ii) _____ [1]

(c) Which ingredient is not required if you use banana leaves when frying food?

_____ [1]

(d) What is one benefit of wrapping rice and curry in banana leaves?

_____ [1]

(e) How do the leaves help other crops when they are growing?

_____ [1]

(f) What are the advantages of using banana leaves as packaging? Give **two** details.

_____

_____ [1]

(g) Why are banana leaves popular as wedding decorations?

_____ [1]

[Total: 8]

Source: Cambridge IGCSE E2L (0510/21) May/June 2009, page 3, Exercise 1

Activity 34

Look at the questions again and underline the key words or phrases in each one.

Activity 35

Write your answers to the questions (Core or Extended).

Activity 36

Look at the four sets of sample answers below. Decide which are the best and worst answers.

(1) **CORE**

(a) bananas, wheat and maize

(b) oil

(c) it adds to the food distinct flavour

(d) because it keep crops away from getting wet

(e) it keep the freshness of the fruits and they prevent the packing materials from getting squashed

(f) it bring to the couple good luck and prosperity

(2) **CORE**

(a) rice, wheat and maize

(b) the ingredient not required is oil

(c) one benefit is it adds a distinct flavour to the food

(d) they keep them from getting wet

(e) the advantages are they retain the freshness of the fruits and they are eco-friendly.

(f) they bring good luck to the couple getting married

(3) **EXTENDED**

(a) rice, wheat and maize

(b) (i) more hygienic

(ii) can be disposed of in an environmentally friendly way

(c) oil

(d) add a distinct flavour

(e) they provide shade

(f) prevent the fruits from getting squashed and it keep the freshness of the fruits

(g) they bring luck and prosperity to the couple getting married

(4) **EXTENDED**

(a) rice, wheat and maize

(b) (i) more hygienic

(ii) can be used as a non-stick frying pan

(c) oil

(d) add a flavour to the food

(e) they provide shelter from the wet

(f) eco-friendly and retain the freshness of the fruit

(g) they bring good luck to the couple getting married

Activity 37

Look at the examiners' comments for the four sets of sample answers in Activity **36**. Match the sets of answers (**1–4**) with the comments below (**a–d**).

a *The answers are short, which is good, and generally contain the important details necessary for a correct answer. However, the candidate has not been exact enough with question (e) and has failed to realise the difference between* shade *and* shelter. *Also, in question (b), the candidate has only scored one mark out of two because of not reading the question carefully.*

b *The answers are short and although the expression is not always correct, the meaning is totally clear. However, question (a) is factually incorrect and the candidate has not taken care with the reading of the first paragraph. The candidate has not realised the difference between* shade *and* shelter *in question (d). Question (e) cannot be given a mark because there is only one correct piece of information and both details need to be correct here to earn one mark.*

c *The candidate has obviously read the text very carefully and given the correct key details for each answer. There are two details supplied whenever the question demands such an answer. In addition, the responses are short and the candidate has taken care to avoid writing more than is necessary.*

d *Question (d) is incorrect because the leaves provide shade (i.e. from the sun) and not shelter from the rain. The candidate is not exact enough with the reading of the text here. In addition, the candidate's answers in (b), (c) and (e) are too long because of the repetition of the wording in the question. This should always be avoided because it wastes time and adds no important detail to the answer.*

Activity 38

The total marks given to the four candidates in Activity **36** were 3, 5, 6 and 8. Match the marks with the sets of answers **1–4**.

EXERCISE 2 – CORE AND EXTENDED

You are going to look at some sample answers from IGCSE students to the Exercise 2 question on page **24**.

Activity 39

Before you read the sample answers and the text in detail, look at the graph. What information does it give you? How does this information link to the title *Soon we may live for 200 years*?

Exercise 2

Read the following article about research into people living longer, and then answer the questions.

Soon we may live for 200 years

The day may come when people will celebrate the start of middle age on their l00th birthday. Some of the world's most eminent experts on ageing have made predictions about average life expectancy – that is the age that you can hope to live to. Those experts say that by the end of this century in some parts of the world people may live to 200 years of age.

From the late 1800s to the present day, the average life span has almost doubled. Some scientists predict a jump of even greater proportions over the next 100 years, thanks to advances in medical science.

Scientists are researching many interesting possibilities at the present time. For example, within the next ten years, they may be able to grow new teeth from stem cells in the laboratory. They are also hoping to develop drugs which can imitate the effects of eating less so that people reduce their calorie intake. This means that people should stay healthier because fewer will be overweight. These scientists are attempting to increase life span by up to 50%. If such changes happen, the world will be dominated by people over 100 years old.

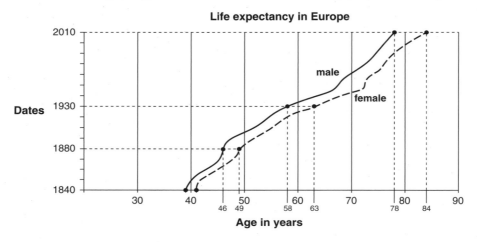

At the present time, the longest recorded human life span is of a Frenchwoman, Jeanne-Louise Calment, who was born in 1875 and died in 1997 at the age of 122 years and 164 days. This is, of course, a real exception, but who knows whether it will be so rare in the future?

In the last century, cleaner living conditions and the discovery of life-saving medicines led to longer life expectancy. A professor of medicine at an American university stated: 'People haven't realised it but with the developments in medical science, we are in a similar position now to increase life expectancy dramatically. At present, as you get older, your cells slowly stop repairing themselves, but with new medical discoveries I think we are going to be able to reverse that process.'

However, other scientists are less convinced. They believe that the human body has a fixed limit on life span that it will not be possible to exceed. One of this group said: 'Living for 200 years is unrealistic. To do that we would have to wipe out things like cancer, heart disease and other major health problems. Despite the huge amount of money being spent on research into these diseases, their complete removal is frustratingly slow.'

Many scientists, however, are excited by the possibilities of a longer life. One expert said: 'How many of us have wanted to do something else with our lives, such as be a novelist, but have not had the time? So much human potential is undiscovered. Perhaps with longer lives, we could start to achieve more of our dreams.'

Source: Cambridge IGCSE E2L (0510/21) May/June 2009, page 4, Exercise 2

Activity 40

Now look at questions **(a)–(j)** below (remember that the final question, **(j)**, is for the Extended paper only*). Which questions require more than one piece of information in your answer? How many marks are available for these questions? Which question asks you to look at the graph in the text?

_____

_____

_____

(a) How has the average life span changed from the late 1800s to the present day?

_____ [1]

(b) What areas of research are scientists undertaking at the moment? Give **two** examples.

(i) _____ [1]

(ii) _____ [1]

(c) What was unusual about Jeanne-Louise Calment?

_____ [1]

(d) What contributed to longer life expectancy in the last century? Give **two** details.

(i) _____ [1]

(ii) _____ [1]

(e) What is the effect of ageing on our body cells?

_____ [1]

(f) According to the graph, what was the difference in life expectancy between men and women in 1930?

_____ [1]

(g) Why do some scientists believe that the human body has a fixed age limit?

_____ [1]

(h) What benefit could we receive from living longer?

_____ [1]

*Also note there is no question here labelled with the letter **(i)** in case it is confused with the first part of questions **(b)** or **(d)** which are labelled with the roman numeral **(i)**. You will find this in other past papers, but future exam papers will probably include the letter **(i)**.

(j) What exactly are some experts predicting about living longer **and** how is a change of eating habits important in achieving this? Give **two** details for each.

Predictions:

(i) _____

(ii) _____

Effects of changes in eating habits:

(i) _____

(ii) _____ [4]

[Total: 14]

Source: Cambridge IGCSE E2L (0510/21) May/June 2009, page 5, Exercise 2

Activity 41

Read the questions again in more detail and underline the key words or phrases in each one.

Activity 42

Write your answers to the questions.

Activity 43

Look at the four sets of sample answers below. Decide which are the best and worst answers.

(1) CORE

(a) it almost doubled

(b) (i) they grow new teeth from stem cells

(ii) develop drugs

(c) lived to be 122 years and 164 days old

(d) (i) cleaner living conditions

(ii) life-saving medicines

(e) cells slowly stop repairing themselves

(f) 5

(g) living for 200 years is unrealistic

(h) that you can achieve more of your dreams

(2) CORE

(a) it doubled

(b) **(i)** they may be able to grow new teeth

(ii) the effects of eating less

(c) that she was very old

(d) **(i)** cleaner living conditions

(ii) discovery of life saving medicines

(e) as you get older your cells slowly stop repairing themselves

(f) women lived longer than men

(g) we would have to wipe out things like cancer, heart disease and other major health problems.

(h) we could start to achieve more of our dreams

(3) EXTENDED

(a) almost doubled

(b) **(i)** growing new teeth from stem cells

(ii) developing drugs to imitate the effects of eating less

(c) longest recorded human lifespan

(d) **(i)** cleaner living conditions

(ii) discovery of life saving medicines

(e) they slowly stop repairing themselves

(f) five years

(g) complete removal of major diseases is slow

(h) we could start to achieve more of our dreams

(j) Predictions:

(i) start middle age on their 100th birthday

(ii) a jump of even greater proportions

Effects of changes in eating habits:

(i) reduce calorie intake

(ii) people should stay healthier

(Continued on page 28)

(4) EXTENDED

(a) it has almost doubled

(b) **(i)** they may be able to grow new teeth

(ii) develop drugs that reduce their calorie intake

(c) she lived from 1885 to 1997

(d) **(i)** cleaner living conditions

(ii) discovery of life saving medicines

(e) as you get older, your cells slowly stop repairing themselves

(f) 5 years

(g) the complete removal of major health problems is slow

(h) perhaps with longer lives we could start to achieve more of our dreams

(j) Predictions:

(i) people may live to 200 years of age

(ii) living for 200 years is unrealistic

Effects of changes in eating habits:

(i) reduce calorie intake

(ii) people stay healthier because fewer people overweight

Activity 44

Look at the examiners' comments for the four sets of sample answers in
Activity **43**. Match the sets of answers (**1–4**) with the comments below (**a–d**).

a *The candidate's understanding of the majority of the text is good, with exact answers.
However, in question (b), the answers are both incomplete (there is no idea of
growing new teeth 'from stem cells') and incorrect, misunderstanding the nature
and purpose of the drugs. The answer in (j) (ii) of the Predictions section is also
not a prediction.*

b *There is a good attempt to give brief answers but in doing so the candidate has left
out some of the key details. For example, the response in question (b) (ii) does not
include important details about the drugs. Similarly, the number '5' in question (f)
is not clear, since there is no indication that this refers to years. Candidates should
always include references to measurements, currencies or other dimensions when
there is a number in the answer.*

c *There has been careful reading of the questions and accurate selection of information from the text. The candidate has recognised all the important details and successfully reduced the answers without losing key words. As a result, the answers are short but exact. The candidate has only lost one mark, in question (j) (ii) of the Predictions section, where the answer does not follow the wording of the question.*

d *There are many instances where the candidate has been careless with the reading of both the text and the questions. For example, the key word* almost *is not included in question (a), although it is clearly in the text. Similarly, in question (f), the candidate has understood the general idea of the graphical information, but has failed to use this precisely in the answer.*

Activity 45

The total marks given to the four candidates in Activity **43** were 6, 5, 11 and 13. Match the marks with the sets of answers **1–4**.

D Exam practice

1 CORE

Exercise 1

Read the following information about an adventure holiday, and then answer the questions on the opposite page.

iTry adventure activities

About iTry Adventures

iTry is for all the family – children to seniors, beginners to advanced adventurers! The activities have been specially chosen to offer a wide range of experiences, appealing to all tastes and abilities. Choose your adventure activity and then match it with one of the following three exciting special options!

Ocean adventure day

One of our most popular adventure days, combining the thrills of coasteering with the excitement of kayaking. Explore the coastline by climbing, jumping from sea cliffs and swimming in the waves. The ultimate in excitement, this activity can be tailored to match your fearlessness and energy levels. Our kayaking sessions explore this superb coastline from a new perspective.

iTry taster day

If you're not sure which activity is best for you, this is a great way to try out three different activities – for all the family from age seven upwards. Start off in the morning on the dizzy heights of the climbing wall. After a short break for lunch, head off to the dry ski slope where your instructor will guide you through the basic skills necessary to get you whizzing down the slope. Then prepare to get wet with lots of fun and games splashing around on the lake.

iTry taster sessions

For those of you who can't spare a whole day, don't worry! Try one of our two-hour adventure tasters. Choose from climbing, skiing or canoeing at 20 euros each – a great bargain!

Note: *All specialist equipment is provided by iTry Adventures. However, you need to bring a towel, a complete change of clothes and shoes that you don't mind getting wet. You will also need to bring a packed lunch, plenty to drink and some sun block.*

Call the booking line 0844 90 22 970
Visit the web www.itry-snowdonia.com

Adapted from iTry tourist leaflet 'Daily adventure taster sessions in Snowdonia', iTry, www.itry-snowdonia.com

(a) What age group is iTry for?

_____ [1]

(b) Apart from coasteering and kayaking, what else can you do on the ocean adventure day? Give **three** details.

_____

_____

_____ [1]

(c) What is the youngest age to join the iTry taster day?

_____ [1]

(d) How can an instructor help you on the dry ski slope?

_____ [1]

(e) How much does it cost for one person to do an iTry taster session?

_____ [1]

(f) Apart from clothes and shoes, what do you need to take with you for an iTry adventure activity? Give **three** details.

_____

_____

_____ [1]

[Total: 6]

Exercise 1

Read the following information about an ape and monkey rescue centre, and then answer the questions on the opposite page.

Monkey World – ape rescue centre

Our 65-acre park is home to over 230 rescued and endangered apes and monkeys. Many have been neglected, kept in unnatural conditions or have experienced unbelievable cruelty. Some are now part of international breeding programmes for endangered species. Here they can all enjoy the company of their own kind in a safe, natural environment.

It's time to talk

We have half-hourly talks by our dedicated monkey and ape keepers – this will be one of the highlights of your visit. The keepers love to share their knowledge, so don't hesitate to ask questions when the talk is completed.

Eat and shop

It's not just the monkeys that get hungry! Our Treetops café has a large outdoor patio, while the Wateringhole café is open during the summer months only. There are also plenty of kiosks selling drinks and ice creams throughout the park.

Party time!

For a true birthday treat, it has to be Monkey World! Our birthday parties are unforgettable – you can make it a full day of fun as they include FREE admission to the park, and party bags for all the kids. And to eat, choose from our 'Jungle Feast' menu of pasta, 100% chicken chunks, premium sausages or fish, or try our organic meals, or how about a 'Vegetarian Jungle Picnic'? Delicious sandwiches, fruit juice, organic cakes and a surprise gift for everyone!

Adopt a monkey or ape

You can help monkeys and apes in danger by adopting one of our family or by giving an adoption as a special present to someone.

As a 'thank you' you will receive a photo of your chosen animal, an adoption certificate and a year's free entry to Monkey World. Visit our Adoption Centre next to the Treetops café if you want to find out more. And remember – all the money you give goes to animal rescue, not to administration.

Adapted from Monkey World tourist leaflet 'Monkey World – where families matter', www.monkeyworld.org

(a) How large is Monkey World?

_____ [1]

(b) How often can you listen to a talk about monkeys and apes?

_____ [1]

(c) When is the Wateringhole café closed?

_____ [1]

(d) If you book a birthday party, what **two** things do you **not** have to pay for?

_____

_____ [2]

(e) What food choice is offered for people who do not eat meat?

_____ [1]

(f) What do you get when you adopt a monkey or ape? Give **two** details.

_____

_____ [1]

(g) Where can you get more information about adopting a monkey or ape?

_____ [1]

[Total: 8]

Exercise 1

Read the following information about hay fever, and then answer the questions on the opposite page.

Your guide to managing hay fever

Runny or blocked nose? Sneezing? Watery eyes? They are all common symptoms of hay fever, although some people also have a sore throat and an annoying cough. Hay fever is an allergic reaction, usually to pollen from flowers and tree blossom (flowers), although other things can cause it too.

What's an allergy?

When you have an allergy, it means that your body is more sensitive to certain substances. If you have hay fever, you're more likely to suffer from the allergy-related conditions of eczema (a skin condition) and asthma (a lung condition that affects breathing). You're also more likely to have hay fever if someone in your family has these conditions.

Hay fever can make you feel miserable. Sleeping can be difficult, and your head may feel strange, making it hard to make decisions.

There are many types of pollen (a type of dust produced by plants). When flowers open in the spring and summer, many hay fever sufferers show the symptoms described above. Many people suffer from the pollen in grass, also in the summer months.

Children and hay fever

Hay fever symptoms can be especially hard for children. They can feel self-conscious about a constantly runny nose and sneezing, and may have to avoid playing outside when the pollen count is high. More importantly, hay fever can affect school performance, which is particularly serious during examination time. The good news for childhood allergy sufferers is that symptoms often lessen or completely disappear during adulthood.

Help yourself

You can't avoid pollen, but here's how you can limit your exposure to it:

1 Check the pollen forecast on the internet, in the newspaper or on the radio or television. If you can, stay indoors with the windows shut on days when the pollen count is high.

2 The peak times for pollen are 7–10 a.m. and 4–7 p.m. Spend as little time outside as possible during these hours.

3 If you have been outside, change your clothes and have a shower to wash the pollen off your skin and hair.

4 Try keeping a hay fever diary so that next year you will know when to start taking your hay fever medicines ahead of the pollen season.

Adapted from Boots information leaflet 'Your guide to managing hayfever', 2007

(a) Give **two** common symptoms of hay fever.

_____

_____ [1]

(b) Where does pollen come from? Name **two** things.

_____

_____ [1]

(c) What other conditions are hay fever sufferers likely to have?

_____ [1]

(d) If you suffer from hay fever, what **two** activities might become a problem?

(i) _____ [1]

(ii) _____ [1]

(e) What might happen to a child's hay fever symptoms as they get older?

_____ [1]

(f) **EXTENDED ONLY**: Give **two** ways in which you can reduce the chance of being affected by pollen.

_____

_____ [2]

[Total: 6 or 8]

Exercise 2

Read the following information about toads in Australia, and then answer the questions on the opposite page.

Toads are arthritic and in pain

Arthritis is an illness that can cause pain and swelling in your bones. Toads, a big problem in the north of Australia, are suffering from painful arthritis in their legs and backbone, a new study has shown. The toads that jump the fastest are more likely to be larger and to have longer legs. But this advantage also has a big drawback – up to 10% of the biggest toads suffer from arthritis.

The large yellow toads, native to South and Central America, were introduced into the north-eastern Australian state of Queensland in 1935 in an attempt to stop beetles and other insects from destroying sugarcane crops. Now up to 200 million of the poisonous toads exist in the country, and they are rapidly spreading through the state of Northern Territory at a rate of up to 60 km a year. The toads can now be found across more than one million square kilometres. The task now facing the country is how to remove the toads. A Venezuelan poison virus was tried in the 1990s but had to be abandoned after it was found to also kill native frog species.

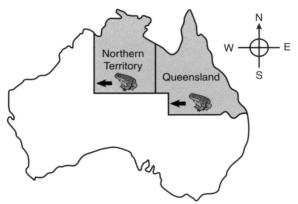

The toads have severely affected ecosystems in Australia. Animals, and sometimes pets, that eat the toads die immediately from their poison, and the toads themselves eat anything they can fit inside their mouth. Furthermore, they soon take over the natural habitats of Australia's native species.

A co-author of the new study, Rick Shine, a professor at the University of Sydney, says that little attention has been given to the problems that toads face. Rick and his colleagues studied nearly 500 toads from Queensland and the Northern Territory and found that those in the latter state were very different. They were active, sprinting down roads and breeding quickly.

According to the results of the study, the fastest toads travel nearly one kilometre a night. Toads with longer legs move faster and travel longer distances, while the others are being left behind. But speed and strength come at a price – arthritis of the legs and backbone due to constant pressure placed on them.

In laboratory tests, the researchers found that after about 15 minutes of hopping, arthritic toads would travel less distance with each hop. But arthritis didn't slow down toads outside the laboratory, the researchers found. These toads are so programmed to move, apparently, that even when in pain the toads travelled as fast and as far as the healthy ones, continuing their relentless march across the landscape.

Rick says: 'Toads are not built to be road runners – they are built to sit around ponds and wet areas. But because they are pushing themselves so hard against their own bodies, they are placing enormous pressure on their bones. Frogs and toads do not normally get arthritis.'

Adapted from 'Cane toads are arthritic and in pain' by Stephanie Peatling, *The Week* (Oman), November 2007, www.freetheweek.com

(a) In which two parts of the body are toads affected by arthritis?

_____ [1]

(b) Why are stronger and faster toads at a disadvantage?

_____ [1]

(c) Where do the large yellow toads originally come from?

_____ [1]

(d) According to the diagram, in which direction are the toads moving quickly?

_____ [1]

(e) What are **two** problems that the toads cause to ecosystems?

_____

_____ [2]

(f) In which state were the more active toads found?

_____ [1]

(g) What happens to the toads with shorter legs? Give **two** details.

_____

_____ [1]

(h) What difference did researchers find between toads with arthritis in the laboratory and outside?

_____

_____ [2]

(i) **EXTENDED ONLY:** Give **four** pieces of information related to the two dates 1935 and the 1990s.

_____

_____

_____

_____ [4]

[Total: 10 or 14]

Exercise 2

Read the following information about mobile (cell) phones, and then answer the questions on the opposite page.

Precious metals in mobile phones

Are you thinking of throwing out your old mobile phone? If you are, then think again. Maybe you should mine it first for gold, silver, copper and other metals used in the electronic components. With the price of metals sky-rocketing, this is a growth industry!

The materials recovered from mobile phones can be used in new electronic parts, and the gold and other precious metals can be sold to jewellers and investors as well as back to manufacturers. They will use the gold in the circuit boards of mobile phones because gold conducts electricity even better than copper. Also, the amount of gold produced from mining it from the ground is about 5 grams per tonne of ore (the rock which contains gold), whereas a tonne of discarded mobile phones can produce as much as 150 grams.

Some countries are extremely large consumers of mobile phones and other electronics, but have few natural resources, such as precious metals. In these countries it makes good economic sense to recycle electronic components instead of throwing them away, because it reduces the need to import more precious metals. In Japan, for example, the population of 128 million uses a mobile phone for an average of two years and eight months. That's a lot of phones being discarded every year, but only about 15% are recycled. This is because people tend not to actually throw away their old phones, but to put them in a drawer or a cupboard and forget about them. One reason for this might be that people are concerned about personal data stored on their mobile phone; another is that people tend to think of a phone as a very personal item. In many countries, the top of the range models are quite expensive to buy. Although some people always want to buy the latest models, most people feel better if they keep their phones as long as possible.

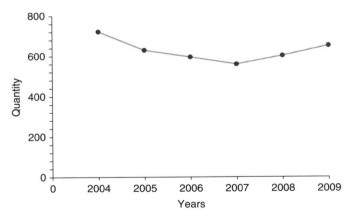

Phones recycled in Japan (tonnes per year)

Nozomu Yamanaka, manager of the Eco-Systems Recycling Company, 80 km southwest of Tokyo, Japan, says: 'To some people old phones and electronics are just a mountain of rubbish, but to my company they are a mountain of gold. However, these days, because of competition from recycling firms in China, we are importing used mobile phones and electronics from other countries, such as Singapore and Indonesia. These electronics contain other metals such as indium, which is a vital product in the production of flat panel televisions and computer screens.'

Adapted from 'Urban miners look for precious metals in cell phones' by Miho Yoshikawa, *Oman Daily Observer*, 28th April 2008

(a) Why should we think twice about throwing out an old mobile phone?

_____ [1]

(b) Give **three** ways in which the valuable metals from mobile phones can be recycled.

_____

_____

_____ [1]

(c) What advantage does gold have over copper?

_____ [1]

(d) How does mining gold from the ground compare to getting it from old mobile phones?

_____ [1]

(e) Why is it a good idea to recycle electronic components in countries which have few natural resources?

_____ [1]

(f) According to the graph, has the annual number of recycled phones in Japan increased or decreased since 2007?

_____ [1]

(g) How is Yamanaka's company's opinion of old mobile phones different from other people's?

_____

_____ [2]

(h) Why is Japan importing used electronic components from other countries?

_____ [1]

(i) What **two** electronic items use indium as an essential component?

_____

_____ [1]

(j) **EXTENDED ONLY:** Why do people tend not to discard their old mobile phones? Give **four** reasons.

_____

_____

_____

_____ [4]

[Total: 10 or 14]

Exercise 2

Read the following information about a boat builder in Cyprus, and then answer the questions on the opposite page.

The last boat builder

If you walk behind the football stadium in the town of Ayia Napa in Cyprus, you would think you've gone back a century, to a period when craftsmen worked day and night, building wooden boats for the local fishermen and other sailors.

Sitting on top of a giant boat, 62-year-old Antonakis Gregoris calls me over, with his hammer in his hand. Antonakis, helped by his son and wife, are working day and night, rebuilding one of his tourist boats that was burned by fire during the summer. The fire destroyed four boats, leaving several families without any income.

Despite the hardships faced after the fire, Antonakis immediately started on the near-impossible task of pulling what remained of the boat, which really was only a small part from the rear end, to a small piece of land overlooking the town, given to him by the local municipality. From there he promised himself to rebuild it from almost nothing.

He is living proof that this old, traditional craft has not been forgotten in Cyprus. His mission is to have his boat finished before the next summer tourist season starts.

'Losing your boat ... it hurts terribly. But that is why we must start again and keep on working, working, working.'

This is the second time that disaster has struck Antonakis. In 2002, he was called a hero when a fire on one of his tourist boats, near Konnos Bay, went out of control.

'When I was helping people get off the boat I was injured and spent three months in hospital, but luckily everybody managed to get off the boat safely, so I was very happy. People sent me gifts and flowers.'

Despite being given no financial aid by the municipality, Antonakis has been overwhelmed by support from friends, family and the municipality, who have literally 'pushed the boat out' to help him.

'The municipality has helped me very much: they have given me electricity and water, and for this help I am so grateful to the mayor and his staff,' he says.

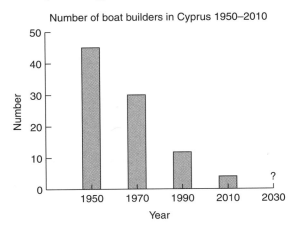

Number of boat builders in Cyprus 1950–2010

Antonakis works obsessively hard. He started this job when he was 10 years old, working with his father in a port on the coast of Cyprus. He has been working in this trade since then. He didn't know that when he began work as an apprentice in the late 1950s he would be one of the very last men to practise this ancient craft.

Sitting outside the small hut given to him by the municipality he says, 'If nobody else learns this type of work, I believe that I will be the last, because I am the youngest boat builder in Cyprus. Everyone else – and there are only three others – is over 70,' he says.

Nowadays, with almost all boats being imported from abroad, there is little demand for locally built vessels, but Antonakis does get the occasional enquiry.

'Most boats come from Egypt and Arabian ports, and some come from Europe. Because there are no special factories or boat yards in Cyprus, mostly people bring boats from outside the country. I have had a few people visit me and ask for boats, but I honestly just don't have the time to make one for somebody else.'

Adapted from 'The last boat builder' by Nathan Morley, *Sunday Mail*, Cyprus, 13th December 2009

(a) Who did the craftsmen build boats for one hundred years ago?

_____ [1]

(b) How many boats were destroyed by the fire during the previous summer?

_____ [1]

(c) How much of Antonakis's boat was left after the fire?

_____ [1]

(d) Why does Antonakis carry on working hard? Give **two** details.

_____

_____ [2]

(e) How many people were injured when Antonakis's tourist boat caught fire in 2002?

_____ [1]

(f) Who has helped Antonakis since the fire on his boat? Give **three** details.

_____ [1]

(g) How many boat builders were there in Cyprus in 1970?

_____ [1]

(h) Why does Antonakis think he will be the last boat builder in Cyprus?

_____ [1]

(i) Why do so few people buy boats built in Cyprus? Give **two** details.

_____

_____ [2]

(j) **EXTENDED ONLY**: Find **four** pieces of evidence in the text to show that Antonakis has been helped by the municipality.

_____

_____

_____

_____ [4]

[Total: 10 or 14]

Exercise 3

In this unit you will learn about Exercise 3, the form-filling exercise in the IGCSE E2L examination, and practise the skills you need.

A Introduction

What is Exercise 3?

Exercise 3 in both the Core and Extended papers is an information transfer activity. This means that you read a text and transfer information from it to a form.

Exercise 3

(1) The Sciapoulos family has won a holiday to Croatia and is interested in visiting Dubrovnik, a region that seems to have all the facilities and attractions the family want.

The Dubrovnik Tourist Office offers a free service to holiday-makers who want to visit the region. If Nina's family completes a questionnaire before the holiday, the Tourist Office can suggest where to stay and what to do in the area. They can also organise travel arrangements.

(3) 19-year-old Nina lives near the capital city of (4) Athens at number 47 Koronis in a suburb called Chalandrion. She lives with her parents and twin (3) brothers, Costas and Demis, who will soon be 17 years old. Her father Dimitris is a professional (2) musician and is often away from home. Since he usually spends so much time rushing from place to place, he would prefer a relaxing holiday with as much swimming as possible. He enjoys staying (2) in hotels. Nina's mother Maria works five days a week in a hospital. She prefers to be more active on holiday and loves walking or playing games on the beach. She does not enjoy sitting and sunbathing.

Imagine you are Nina Sciapoulos. Fill in the form, using the information above.

Holiday Trip Questionnaire
SECTION A PERSONAL DETAILS

Family name:

_____ (1)

Parent(s): first name(s):

_____ (2)

_____

Children: first name(s):

_____ Age: _____ (3)

_____ Age: _____

_____ Age: _____

Family address: _____ (4)

_____

_____

Source: Cambridge IGCSE E2L (0510/22) May/June 2008, page 6, Exercise 3

How many marks are there?

In the Core paper there are ten marks for this exercise, while in the Extended paper there are eight.

In the first part of both the Core and Extended papers there are six marks available (12 marks divided by 2 to give a total of 6; there are no half marks). In the final section of the Core paper you have to write two sentences for a possible two marks per sentence (four marks available in total). In the Extended paper you only need to write one sentence for the two marks available.

What are the assessment objectives?

For the Core and Extended papers, you are assessed on your ability to:
- understand and respond to information presented in a variety of forms (Reading assessment objective 1)
- select and organise material relevant to specific purposes (R2)
- communicate clearly, accurately and appropriately (Writing assessment objective 1)
- observe conventions (rules) of paragraphing, punctuation and spelling (W5).

For the Extended paper, Reading assessment objective 4 is also included:
- infer information from texts (R4).

Check!

What do you think these phrases mean?

1 information presented in a variety of forms
2 select and organise material
3 communicate clearly, accurately and appropriately
4 infer information
5 observe conventions

Match the phrases above with the advice below.

a Your writing should follow the rules.
b Sometimes when you read you may need to guess what something means.
c The things you write should be easy to read and understand.
d You need to choose the right information from the texts and arrange it correctly.
e You will read texts taken from advertisements, articles, magazines, reports, etc.

What does Exercise 3 look like?

In the examination paper you will see a text on the left-hand page and a form to fill in on the right-hand page. The form is divided into sections: A, B, C, and so on; each section asks you for a different type of information from the text. The final section is for writing a sentence based on the text. In the Core paper you need to write **two** sentences.

What's the difference between the Core and Extended papers?

Exercise 3

Check!

Complete the information in the box with the words and phrases below.

> final section   slightly shorter   **two** sentences   Core

> The main difference is that the Core text is _____ than
> the Extended text. In the _____ paper you need to write
> _____ in the _____ .

What do I have to do?

The question usually says something like:

> Imagine you are (*the person in the text*). Fill in the form on the opposite page, using the
> information above.

You need to find the correct information in the text and transfer it to the form. Remember that the text gives information about one person, or one main person, and other people in the third person (*she, he, they*). In order to fill in the form, you have to imagine that you are the main person and fill in the form in the first/main person (*I*).

What do I need to know?

It is very important in Exercise 3 that you write addresses and fill in the form in the correct way. Also, when you transfer information from the text to the form, correct spelling is very important. In the final section in the Core paper, you need to write **two** sentences; in the Extended paper, you need to write **one** sentence. It is also important to make sure you understand the difference between underlining, circling, ticking and deleting, and to notice if the question asks you to write in capital letters.

Check!

Match the words with the examples.

deleting	LONDON
underlining	(14–16 years)
circling	football
ticking	breakfast
capital letters	male ✓

Remember!

- The spelling of every word must be correct.
- Underlining means that you must <u>underline</u> and not (circle.)
- Tick = ✓
- The information in the text may not be given in the order on the form.
- Only write **one** sentence 12–20 words (Extended).
- Write **two** sentences (Core).
- There is no word limit for the two sentences in the Core paper.
- Don't forget to write in CAPITALS if the questions asks you to.

B Preparation

Addresses are written in different ways across the world. How is an address written in your country? What information comes first, second, and so on?

Activity 1

Write your own name and address on this envelope.

In Italy, addresses are written like this:

Mario Rossi
Via Appia Nuova 287
00183 Roma RM

In the USA, like this:

Mr John Smith
123 Main Street
Beverly Hills, CA 90201

In the UK, like this:

Ms Maria Windsor
3 High Street
Manchester
M22 3DR

In Japan, the order of information is very different:

Postcode
Name region and name of block
Address
Name of receiver

And in Poland:

PARAFIA RZYSKO KATOLICKA
LUBNO
36-065 DYNOW
woj. PODKARPACKIE
POLAND

Activity 2

Are any of the addresses written the same way as yours in Activity 1? How are they the same or different?

_____

_____

Activity 3

Look at this information, which is in the wrong order. What is the best order for someone's name and address, using the UK style?

a   town/village, city, prefecture/state/province

b   name of the building, like an apartment building, and room number (if necessary)

c   postal code / zip code, country

d   house number, street

e   person's name

In Exercise 3 of the IGCSE examination you may be asked to transfer a person's name and address from the text to the form. It is important that you write the information in the correct way. Remember that the information may be given in a different order in the text.

Activity 4

Read the short text below and underline the information which matches with **a–d** from Activity **3** above. Label the information in the text **a–d**.

> Giovanni Politti is an Italian citizen who was born in Milan but now lives in Rome. He lives in via Colosseo at building 56A, in apartment 311. The postal code for his address is 00876.

Activity 5

Now fill in the form using the information about Giovanni.

Family name: _____

First name: _____

Full address: _____

_____

_____

Sometimes the question asks for contact details such as an email address and a telephone number as well as a date of birth. It is important that you copy these details correctly from the text onto the form – if you make a mistake with numbers or spelling, you will not be given the marks.

Activity 6

The text below is an extract from an IGCSE Extended paper Exercise 3. Read the text and the filled-in form that follows. What is wrong with the answer given?

19-year-old Nina Sciapoulos, who comes from Greece, lives near the capital city of Athens at number 47 Koronis in a suburb called Chalandrion. The whole family can be contacted by phone at home on 143769045 but the only time when the family can definitely be reached is in the evening after 19:00 hours. Being contacted by email at sciapo2@systema.gr is preferable for the family.

Adapted from Cambridge IGCSE E2L (0510/22) May/June 2008, page 6, Exercise 3

First name: Sciapoulos

Family name: Nina

Full address: Athens, at number 47 Kornis, Greece, Chalandrion

Email: sciapou2@systema.gr

Telephone: 1437690045

Activity 7

Read the extract in Activity **6** again and fill in the blank form correctly.

First name: _____

Family name: _____

Full address: _____

Email: _____

Telephone: _____

Activity 8

Look at this second extract from the same text. What information does it give? Read the text and complete the list which follows.

> With regard to accommodation, they are happy with their father's choice. They don't like to eat in local restaurants and would prefer to take all their meals at the hotel. Nina's mother is allergic to milk products but the other members of the family are happy to eat all types of food.
>
> The family's preferred method of travel is by train. They would like the Tourist Office to suggest an itinerary where they travel through the night. They wish to start their holiday in the middle of the week, certainly not at the weekends when it is too crowded. All of them want to return about two weeks later, again overnight. They do not intend to leave the hotel very often and will not need to hire a car or reserve any excursions in advance. They do want to have a local guide in the region in order to do some sightseeing.
>
> Adapted from Cambridge IGCSE E2L (0510/22) May/June 2008, page 6, Exercise 3

The text provides information about …

accommodation

meals

_____

_____

_____

Activity 9

Look at this form based on the text in Activity **8**. What is wrong with it?

SECTION B HOLIDAY DETAILS

Accommodation: (please tick your preference)

[X] Hotel   [ ] Apartment   [ ] Camping

Travel: (please tick your preference)

[ ] Car   [X] Aeroplane   [X] Train

Preferred departure day: (please circle)

Sunday   ✓ Wednesday   Saturday

Preferred departure time: (please circle)

Morning   ✓ Afternoon   Evening

Other requirements: (please delete) **Note:** these must be booked in advance

Car hire Yes / (No)   Guide services ~~Yes~~ / No

Read the text in Activity **8** again and fill in the blank form.

SECTION B HOLIDAY DETAILS

Accommodation: (please tick your preference)

☐ Hotel   ☐ Apartment   ☐ Camping

Travel: (please tick your preference)

☐ Car   ☐ Aeroplane   ☐ Train

Preferred departure day: (please circle)

    Sunday   Wednesday   Saturday

Preferred departure time: (please circle)

    Morning   Afternoon   Evening

Other requirements: (please delete) **Note:** these must be booked in advance

Car hire Yes / No   Guide services Yes / No

Remember!

In the final section of Exercise 3 you have to write **one** sentence in the Extended paper and **two** sentences in the Core paper. For the Extended paper, the sentence must

- be one sentence with no full stops in the middle
- be between 12 and 20 words (21 words will give you zero marks)
- be written in the first person – use first-person verbs and possessive adjectives *my* and *our*
- be based on the content in the text, not on your own personal details
- begin with a capital letter and end with a full stop and must not begin with *and*.

Read the question below and then look back at the text in Activity **8** again.

> In the space below write one sentence of between 12 and 20 words giving details of any dietary requirements.

Now look at these answers to the question. What is wrong with them?

a   None of them has any dietary requirements except for Nina's mother who is allergic to milk products.

b   My whole family is happy to eat all types of food but my mother is allergic to milk products and can't eat them.

c   Everyone in my family eats anything. However my mum can't eat milk products.

d   Only my mum — she can't eat milk products.

e   I can't eat fish, and my dad is a vegetarian, just like my mum. She can't eat milk products either.

C   Exam focus

You are going to look at some sample answers from IGCSE students to the following question:

Exercise 3

(1) James Wheeler, who will be 19 next month, lives in Birmingham, England, at 12 Russell Street. Last year, during his summer vacation, he worked as a volunteer at a camp in France teaching sports activities to children aged 9 to 11. Some of the children were from France so James had the opportunity to practise and improve his French language skills. A small percentage of children came from Germany and Holland but the largest number by far were British. The camp was situated in a wooded area in the heart of the countryside but close to the local village and a long, sandy beach.

(2) The days at the camp were long and James had to get up at 6.30 a.m. and was not usually in bed before midnight. He often had no time to eat lunch, except perhaps for a sandwich which he ate while he was working, but neither of these was a problem to James.

(3) He spent a total of 35 days at the camp and taught swimming in the morning and basketball in the afternoon. He also spent his evenings with young people, playing games, watching videos and singing. One of the reasons he was accepted for the post was because he can play the guitar very well and generally his happiest times during the day were after dinner when the whole group went to the beach and chatted and sang.

(4) It was his first experience of this type of work and he was impressed by the group size, where there was one teacher to eight children. He remembered his days at school when the class sizes were usually about 45 children for each teacher and he had considered it to be such a difficult profession.

(5) There were two main disadvantages. Firstly, he had to work hard in his spare time in a local supermarket to pay for his travel to the camp. He worked at least one evening per week and sometimes on Saturdays and Sundays to earn the money he needed, and this made him very tired. Secondly, when he first arrived at the camp he was homesick but he forgot that as soon as he started working with the children. Despite these problems, he would like to return next summer but would prefer to teach water sports and work with older children.

(6) The whole experience has made him think seriously about teaching as a job in the future. But, at the moment, his immediate priority is to start his course of studies at university in England.

(7) After the summer camp, the organisation that recruits the volunteers contacted James in order to find out his opinion of his experiences at the camp.

Imagine you are James Wheeler. Fill out the feedback form, using the information above.

Source: Cambridge IGCSE E2L (0510/02) May/June 2006, page 6, Exercise 3

Activity 12

Before you read the sample answers, read the question carefully. For each paragraph, **1–7**, make a note of the key points of information it contains.

Paragraph 1 – family name, age, address, previous volunteer work, ... _____

Paragraph 2 – _____

Paragraph 3 – _____

Paragraph 4 – _____

Paragraph 5 – _____

Paragraph 6 – _____

Paragraph 7 – _____

Activity 13

Look at the volunteer feedback form.

VOLUNTEER FEEDBACK FORM

SECTION A

Surname _____ Initial _____

Address _____

_____

_____

Age _____

Time spent at camp (*please circle one*)

less than one month / one to two months / more than two months

Activities taught (*please underline*)

Water sports, Swimming, Volleyball, Badminton, Basketball

Age group taught (*please circle one*)

ages 7–9 / ages 9–11 / ages 11–13

Number of children in group _____

Most students came from (*name the country*)

_____

Did you experience any problems at the camp?

_____

Would you like to work at the camp in the future?
(*please delete one*)

Yes/No

What would your preferences be for any future work?

1 _____

2 _____

SECTION B

In the space below, write **one** sentence of 12–20 words about how your experiences at the camp have influenced your career plans.

_____

_____

Source: Cambridge IGCSE E2L (0510/02) May/June 2006, page 7, Exercise 3

Match the questions on the form with the correct paragraphs in the text.

Example:

Surname and Initial – paragraph 1

Address and Age – paragraph 1

Time spent at camp – _____

_____

_____

_____

_____

_____

Activity 14

Look at the three sample answers below. Decide which are the best and worst answers.

①
VOLUNTEER FEEDBACK FORM

SECTION A

Surname _Wheeler_   Initial _J_

Address   _12 Russell Street_

Birmingham

England

Age   _18_

Time spent at camp (*please circle one*)

less than one month /(one to two months)/ more than two months

Activities taught (*please underline*)

Water sports, <u>Swimming</u>, Volleyball, Badminton, <u>Basketball</u>

Age group taught (*please circle one*)

ages 7–9 /(ages 9–11)/ ages 11–13

Number of children in group _8_

Most students came from (*name the country*)

Britain

Did you experience any problems at the camp?

Homesick

Would you like to work at the camp in the future? (*please delete one*)

Yes/~~No~~

What would your preferences be for any future work?

1 _Teach water sports_

2 _Working with children_

SECTION B

In the space below, write **one** sentence of 12–20 words about how your preparations at the camp have influenced your career plans.

The whole experience has made me think

seriously about teaching as a job in the future.

(2)

VOLUNTEER FEEDBACK FORM

SECTION A

Surname Wheeler   Initial J W

Address 12 Russell Street

Birmingham

England

Age   18

Time spent at camp (*please circle one*)

less than one month / <u>one to two months</u> / more than two months

Activities taught (*please underline*)

Water sports, <u>Swimming</u>, Volleyball, Badminton, <u>Basketball</u>

Age group taught (*please circle one*)

ages 7–9 / (ages 9–11) / ages 11–13

Number of children in group 8

Most students came from (*name the country*)

British

Did you experience any problems at the camp?

I had to work hard in my spare time

Would you like to work at the camp in the future? (*please delete one*)

Yes/~~No~~

What would your preferences be for any future work?

1 Teach water sports

2 Start a course of studies at university

SECTION B

In the space below, write **one** sentence of 12–20 words about how your preparations at the camp have influenced your career plans.

The experience at the camp has made me think seriosly about teching as a job when I am in England.

---

(3)

VOLUNTEER FEEDBACK FORM

SECTION A

Surname Wheeler   Initial J W

Address In Birmingham, England at

12 Russell Street

Age   18

Time spent at camp (*please circle one*)

less than one month / (one to two months) / more than two months

Activities taught (*please underline*)

Water sports, <u>Swimming</u>, Volleyball, Badminton, <u>Basketball</u>

Age group taught (*please circle one*)

(ages 7–9) / ages 9–11 / ages 11–13

Number of children in group 45

Most students came from (*name the country*)

British

Did you experience any problems at the camp?

He was homesick

Would you like to work at the camp in the future? (*please delete one*)

Yes/<u>No</u>

What would your preferences be for any future work?

1 I would like to return next summer

2 I would prefer to teach water spots

SECTION B

In the space below, write **one** sentence of 12–20 words about how your preparations at the camp have influenced your career plans.

My whole experiance at the summer camp has made me thing seriously about teaching as a job in the future in England.

Activity 15

Look at the examiners' comments for the three sample answers in Activity **14**. Match the answers (**1–3**) with the comments below (**a–c**).

a *In Section A, the candidate made eight mistakes. They did not understand* initial *and the correct wording and order of an address. They did not change* British *in the text to* Britain *on the form. Two pieces of information were incorrect. There was underlining instead of deleting, a spelling mistake and use of the third person* he. *In Section B, no marks were given as there were too many words.*

b *In Section A, the candidate understands the difference between underlining, deleting and circling and how to write a name and address. They have answered all the questions except one correctly: a mark was not given for the final response in Section A because it contained no idea of* older. *In Section B, the sentence gave the correct information, was within the word limit and had no grammar mistakes. It got maximum marks.*

c *In Section A, the candidate made five mistakes. They did not understand the word* initial, *and there was underlining instead of circling. They did not change* British *in the text to* Britain *in the form, and there was some incorrect information in the final answers. The candidate could avoid these mistakes by more careful reading of the form. In Section B, the sentence gave the correct information and was within the word limit, but there were two spelling errors, and so the sentence only got one mark.*

Exercise 3

Maria Alexandrou, who lives in Cyprus, was 16 last birthday. She wants to join a local sports club where she can play football, her favourite sport, as well as other sports such as basketball and volleyball. The sports club also offers tennis and gymnastics, but she has never tried these.

Maria lives in Nicosia, the capital of Cyprus, at 9 Edesis Street in an area called Kaimakli. Her post code is 1022. The sports club is not far away from her house, in an area called Ajlantzia, and she can ride there on her bike in ten minutes. Her mobile number is 99386772 and her house telephone number is 22435060. Maria's email address is mariaa@cymail.eu.

Maria is very keen on football and has been in the junior girls' team at her school for three years now, but she wants to improve her ball technique. Maria usually plays in attack, on the left. In the future Maria would like to play in a senior team and travel abroad to play teams in different countries. She also enjoys basketball and volleyball, but plays these for fun and if the weather is too bad for playing football outside. In addition, in the summer months, she likes to go swimming.

Because Maria has a lot of school work, she can only visit the club on one evening a week, on either Tuesday or Wednesday, and on Saturdays. Maria has a part-time job on Saturday afternoons and evenings in a local sports shop, so she can only visit the club on Saturday morning.

Maria knows that the sports club offers various discounts for students, depending on how often they visit the club. For people who visit the club up to twice a week, the weekly fee is 10 euros; for up to five visits a week the fee is 15 euros; and if you want to use the club six or seven times a week the fee is 20 euros. For students there is a 50% discount on these prices. However, students must provide proof of identity: either a student card or a letter from a teacher. Maria recently lost her school bag with her student card in it, so she is going to ask her teacher to write a letter to the sports club.

Imagine you are Maria. Fill in the form on the opposite page, using the information above.

Sports club membership form

SECTION A – Personal details

Full name: _____

Address: _____

Email: _____   Mobile: _____

Age next birthday: _____

SECTION B – Sports

Please tick your preferred sport (only **one**):

☐ gymnastics ☐ tennis ☐ football ☐ swimming ☐ basketball ☐ volleyball

Give details of experience in your preferred sport:

_____

Please tick any other sports which you enjoy:

☐ gymnastics ☐ tennis ☐ football ☐ swimming ☐ basketball ☐ volleyball

SECTION C – Days, times & fees

On which days do you want to visit the club? Please circle all that apply.

Mon   Tue   Wed   Thu   Fri   Sat   Sun

At what time do you want to visit the club? Please circle all that apply.

Morning   Afternoon   Evening

Please tick the weekly fee which applies to you.

☐ 10 euros   ☐ 15 euros   ☐ 20 euros

Are you applying for a student discount? Please delete.

YES / NO

What proof of identity are you providing? Please circle.

Letter   Student card

SECTION D

In the space below, write **one** sentence about how you will travel to the club and **one** sentence about your plans for the future.

_____

_____

_____

_____

[Total: 10]

Exercise 3

Exercise 3

Kamal Jawali is a 19-year-old Saudi Arabian student who has just returned from a holiday in Egypt with his family. He has been asked by the company which booked the holiday to give them some feedback. Kamal lives with his parents and his 15-year-old twin sisters in Riyadh in Apartment 698, Block F3, Al Fazari Street. His sisters' names are Fatma and Noora, and his father is called Ahmed and his mother is Jamila. Kamal's email address is jawali@saudi.email.net and his mobile phone is 12398754. The family's home number is 38219587.

The family had their holiday from 25th July to 3rd August at the Regent Hotel in the centre of Cairo. They booked two rooms: a double room for Kamal and his father, and a family room for Kamal's mother and his two sisters. Breakfast was included in the hotel accommodation, and Noora's special diet was not a problem. For lunch and dinner, the family went to local restaurants in Cairo.

Kamal's father had asked for the hotel to arrange transport from the airport when the family arrived on the early flight from Riyadh at 10.30 a.m. Unfortunately, due to problems with traffic, the car arrived too late and so they took a Cairo taxi to the hotel instead. For the return trip to the airport during the evening of 3rd August, the hotel transport was on time.

The hotel provided a range of facilities for its guests, including a gym, outdoor pool, and spa. Kamal's father used the gym most days, while Kamal, who loves swimming, was a regular visitor to the hotel's pool. However, on two days, the pool was closed for maintenance work and he was disappointed by this. Kamal's father also used the business centre to keep in touch with his work back home. Also, the whole family often checked their emails there, despite the fact that the internet did not work all the time.

Daily tours of Cairo and the surrounding area were offered by the hotel, and the family took advantage of several of these. In particular they enjoyed the evening trip to the sound and light show at the Pyramids of Giza, but the best thing they did was to visit the Egyptian Museum. Because there is so much to see, Kamal's father asked the hotel to arrange a tour of the museum with a guide. The family also visited the Coptic area of Cairo, but because of the crowds of tourists they did not get to see very much of interest. They did this particular tour on their own, without the help of the hotel.

Imagine you are Kamal Jawali. Fill in the holiday feedback form on the opposite page, using the information above.

Holiday feedback form

SECTION A – Personal details

Family name: _____

Adults' (18+) first names: _____

Home address: _____

Email: _____ Home phone: _____

SECTION B – Holiday details

Name of hotel and destination: _____

Travel dates from _____ to _____

Did you arrange transport from the airport to the hotel? (*please delete*)

    YES / NO

Was this service satisfactory? If not, please give brief details of any problem.

_____

Details of rooms booked (*number and type*):

_____

Did you eat in the hotel? (*please circle all that apply*)

    BREAKFAST   LUNCH   DINNER

SECTION C – Hotel facilities

Which facilities did you and your family use? (*please tick all that apply*)

    GYM ☐   SPA ☐   POOL ☐

    BUSINESS CENTRE ☐   GIFT SHOP ☐

Did the hotel arrange any tours for you? (*please delete*) YES / NO

If YES, which ones? (*please tick all that apply*)

    PYRAMIDS ☐   COPTIC AREA ☐   EGYPTIAN MUSEUM ☐

SECTION D

In the space below, write **one** sentence of between 12 and 20 words, describing your biggest disappointment with your holiday.

_____

_____

[Total: 8]

Exercise 3

Gina Trasmundi lives with her parents and her twin brother in a small house in Catania, Italy. Last birthday she was sixteen years old and she has decided that she would like to do some voluntary work at the weekends.

Gina studied at the Catania International Secondary School (CISS) in Via Mazzoni, not far from her house at Via Carlotti 63. Before attending CISS, Gina was a student at the local Catania Primary School from 1999 to 2004. She started at CISS in September 2004 and in May 2010 she took and passed six IGCSEs: English as a Second Language, Italian, Art, Geography, Sociology and Maths. She left CISS in June 2010 and has now just started her A Levels at Catania International College (CIC) in Geography, Sociology and English as a Second Language. Also, Gina was the student president of her school for two years from 2007 to 2009, and was the secretary for the school's environment group for one year before that.

Gina is very interested in the environment, and in particular the area around her home in Catania, which suffers from severe water shortages most years. She has already researched the problem during her time as secretary of the environment group, and she organised several visits to the school by local water experts.

Now Gina would like to work as a volunteer for Our Catania, a local environmental group which is particularly concerned with saving water and making people aware of how precious it is as a natural resource. Because of her heavy A Level schedule at CIC, Gina has decided that she can only volunteer for work at the weekends, and preferably on Saturday mornings, although she could work on Sunday afternoons too. She believes that she can find other people of her age at CIC who would also like to volunteer.

Gina is a keen artist and could design posters and leaflets for Our Catania. Furthermore, she got a grade A in her English IGCSE and so would be able to do translation work for the group. Her email is ginatras@itmail.ity and her mobile/cell number is 59381765.

Imagine you are Gina Trasmundi. Fill in the application form on the opposite page, using the information above.

Our Catania volunteer work application form

Section A – Personal details

Full name: _____

Home address: _____

Email: _____ Mobile/Cell number: _____

Section B – Education

Present school/college: _____

What subjects are you currently studying? _____

Please list **all** the previous schools you have attended, with dates.

1 _____

2 _____

What qualifications do you have? (*Please tick as appropriate*)

IGCSEs ☐   A Levels ☐   Other ☐

Number of passes: _____

Positions of responsibility at school/college:

_____

Section C – Volunteer work

When are you available to work with Our Catania? Please circle your
preferred day and time:

Monday – Friday	Saturday	Sunday
Mornings	Afternoons	Evenings

What other special skills can you offer Our Catania?

_____

Section D

In the space below, write **one** sentence of between 12 and 20 words, saying
why it is important for you to join Our Catania.

_____

_____

[Total: 8]

Exercise 4

In this unit you will learn about Exercise 4, the note-making exercise in the IGCSE E2L examination, and practise the skills you need.

A Introduction

What is Exercise 4?

Exercise 4 in both the Core and Extended papers is a note-making activity. This means that you read a text, take important information from it and write the information in note form.

Exercise 4

Read the following passage about a young mountaineer, and then complete the notes opposite.

① *The past few days have seen another mountaineering record smashed by 22-year-old Jake Meyer. Last year, 2007, he became the youngest Briton to stand on Everest's summit. In the process he became the youngest man in the world to climb the Seven Summits, the highest mountains in each of the seven continents. He is one of the fastest in the world at reaching the top of every mountain he climbs.*

② His training programme is rather unusual because he relies very heavily on his youth and 'feeling good' when out in the hills and mountains. 'I know what it's like to walk until my legs feel like they are on fire, but I have to keep going so that the pain will subside. ② It isn't about the speed you go, but rather about minimising the number of stops you take,' he explained. 'If you stop for only one minute it can easily turn into fifteen minutes which could lose you a kilometre.' Jake added, ② 'I constantly set myself targets of a little bit further each time I go out training. Also I've had to fit this in around my exams. I'm studying environmental geo-science at university and I need to make sure I pass!'

In his latest challenge, he beat the existing speed record for climbing the highest peak in each of the 48 continental states of America. ③ He faced not only the dangers of altitude, but the very real threat of attack by bears or snakes and, of course, in driving from coast to coast, the worry of road accidents. For this challenge, speed was vital.

You are preparing to give a short talk to your hill-walking group about Jake Meyer. Prepare some notes to use as the basis of your talk.

Make your notes under each heading.

Jake's achievements
- .... ①
- ....
- ....

Jake's training details
- .... ②
- ....
- ....

Dangers encountered on his latest challenge
- .... ③
- ....

[Total: 8]

Source: Cambridge IGCSE E2L (0510/21) May/June 2008, pages 8–9, Exercise 4

How many marks are there?

In the Core paper there are six marks for this exercise, while in the Extended paper there are eight. Each correct note is given one mark.

What are the assessment objectives?

For both the Core and Extended papers, you are assessed on your ability to:

- understand and respond to information presented in a variety of forms (Reading assessment objective 1)
- select and organise material relevant to specific purposes (R2)
- recognise, understand and distinguish between facts, ideas and opinions (R3).

Note that there are **no** writing objectives for this question. This means that your **reading skills** are being tested, **not** your writing skills. However, make sure the examiner can understand you; your notes must make sense!

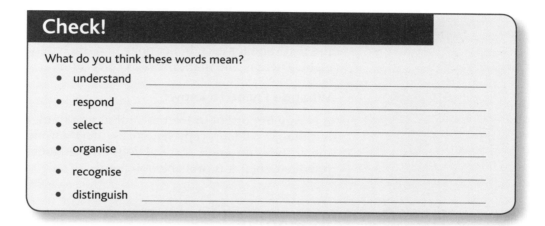

Check!

What do you think these words mean?

- understand _____
- respond _____
- select _____
- organise _____
- recognise _____
- distinguish _____

What does Exercise 4 look like?

In the examination paper you will see a text on the left-hand page and a bulleted list to complete on the right-hand page. The list is divided into sections with different headings which make up the note-making form.

What's the difference between the Core and Extended papers?

Check!

Complete the information in the box with the words and phrases below.

find eight points   difference   differences   the same   exactly   six points

There are no big _____ between the two papers. The text
is _____ the same, and the task you have to complete is
also _____ . The only _____ is that
in the Core paper you need to find _____ , whereas in the
Extended paper you need to _____ .

It is also important to remember that in the Core paper Exercise 4 is linked to Exercise 5, but in the Extended paper it is not. See the unit on Exercise 5 for more information.

What do I have to do?

The task for Exercise 4 is making **notes**. Examiners do not want to see how well you can write a sentence. That is tested in Exercises 5, 6 and 7.

The question explains what the text is about:

> Read the speech by the mayor of a large city who is talking about his ideas to encourage recycling the waste that we currently throw away.

and what you have to do:

> You are a reporter writing an article about the mayor's speech. Prepare some notes to use as the basis for your article.

Source: Cambridge IGCSE E2L (paper 2) May/June 2006, page 9, Exercise 4

You need to find the information in the text and transfer it to the note-making form, below the correct heading. Your answers here should be short and do not have to contain a verb. In the Core paper you need to find six points in the text (one for each bullet point); in the Extended paper you need to find eight. There is one mark for each correct point.

What do I need to know?

It is very important in Exercise 4 that you think about how long your answer is. Some candidates copy sentences directly from the text without putting the answers into note form. If your answer goes beyond the line or the space provided, then it is probably too long.

Remember!

- Keep your answers short and make sure they make sense.
- Make sure you only write **one** point (piece of information) on each line.
- Do **not** repeat the same information, even if you use different words.
- Read and underline the section headings **before** reading the text.
- Transfer information carefully.
- In the Core paper only, Exercise 4 is linked to Exercise 5.
- It is your reading skills that are being tested, **not** your writing skills.

B Preparation

Look at this part of a text from an IGCSE examination paper Exercise 4:

I wonder if you have ever seen a landfill site? Over one million tons of waste each year is deposited in landfill sites around this city. As this figure grows ever larger, we are becoming more concerned about toxic compounds entering the groundwater system. We really don't know how much damage we are all doing. And because the waste is buried, we think that the problem is buried too. We do, of course, take great care to line waste collection points with protective material so that there isn't any leakage, but it does happen.

Medical research is now suggesting that there is a small risk of birth defects in the population living within a 2 kilometre radius of a landfill site. It's not proven yet, but this is a worrying suggestion. Those people living near to a site also report occasional unpleasant smells, even though a deodoriser is used on the perimeter of the sites to neutralise the smells.

Source: Cambridge IGCSE E2L (0510/02) May/June 2006, page 8, Exercise 4

What is the main topic in the two paragraphs of the text? What do you think you will have to write notes about? Choose from this list:

- financial motivation for recycling waste
- medical research about pollution
- problems associated with landfill sites
- action already being taken to reduce problems on the sites
- groundwater systems.

Look at these student answers. What's wrong with them?

Problems associated with landfill sites

- We are becoming concerned about toxic compounds entering the groundwater system.
- We use protective material to line waste collection points with protective material so that there isn't any leakage.
- There is a small risk of birth defects in the population living within a two kilometre radius of a landfill site.

Activity 3

Rewrite the answers in Activity **2** so that they are shorter and clearer.

_____

_____

_____

Activity 4

Look at this student answer. What's wrong with it? Give reasons.

> **Problems associated with landfill sites**
>
> • Leakage and toxic compounds entering the groundwater system. _____

Activity 5

Rewrite the answer in Activity **4**. Remember to look carefully at the text to find the important points, and then separate them. Don't forget that sometimes just one word is enough to get a mark.

_____

Activity 6

Look at this student answer. What's wrong with it? Give reasons.

> **Problems associated with landfill sites**
>
> • unpleasant smells _____
>
> • odours _____

Activity 7

The two answers in Activity **6** express the same idea, but use different words. The same point may be repeated with different words in a text so be careful that your answers each refer to a separate point. Rewrite the answers in Activity **6** giving a separate point for the second bullet.

_____

_____

Activity 8

Look at this student answer. What's wrong with it? Give reasons.

Problems associated with landfill sites

- lined waste collection points
- deodoriser used

Activity 9

Which of the suggested section headings listed in Activity **1** relates to the answers in Activity **8**? Remember to read the section headings and underline information in the text related to them; this will make you focus on the important information.

Activity 10

Look at this student answer. What's wrong with it? Give reasons.

Problems associated with landfill sites

- there isn't any leakage
- population living within a two kilometre radius

Activity 11

Many students find the correct idea or details in the text but then do not get any marks because they do not transfer the information to the form correctly. Rewrite or change the answers in Activity **10** so they are correct.

Activity 12

Look at the three section headings that were used in this examination question.

a   Problems associated with landfill sites

b   Measures already in place to reduce problems on the sites

c   Financial incentives (motivation) to recycle waste

Now read the whole text on page **68**. For each paragraph, decide whether there is any information that relates to each of the section headings. Complete the second column of the table on page **69** by noting the heading number: **a**, **b**, or **c**. Don't worry about the final column for the moment.

Exercise 4

Read the speech by the mayor of a large city who is talking about his ideas to encourage recycling the waste that we currently throw away.

Mayor's speech

(1) Good morning to you all. It's nice to be here today to talk to you about the vital need to manage our waste in a better way.

(2) Did you know that about 73% of household waste in this city is landfilled, buried in a hole in the ground, usually outside the city? Around 20% is burned, and only 7% is recycled. With landfill sites filling up, and public unease about incineration growing, something will have to change soon.

(3) I wonder if you have ever seen a landfill site? Over one million tons of waste each year is deposited in landfill sites around this city. This is not a pretty sight. As this figure grows ever larger, we are becoming more concerned about toxic compounds entering the groundwater system. We really don't know how much damage we are all doing. And because the waste is buried, we think that the problem is buried too. We do, of course, take great care to line the waste collection points with protective material so that there isn't any leakage, but it does happen.

(4) Medical research is now suggesting that there is a small risk of birth defects in the population living within a 2 kilometre radius of a landfill site. It's not proven yet, but this is a worrying suggestion. Those people living near to a site also report occasional unpleasant smells, even though a deodoriser is used on the perimeter of the sites to neutralise smells.

(5) It does seem fairly simple for us to address our growing waste mountain. If we could make more people aware of this problem and how relatively easy it is to reduce waste, we could all live in a cleaner environment.

(6) I am hoping that we can encourage people to separate waste for recycling. For example, tax reductions will be given to those who consistently sort their waste out into paper, plastic, glass and green material. We should use financial benefits to encourage more people to take notice of how seriously we regard this problem. We could introduce educational projects for schoolchildren to help raise the profile of waste management among the younger generation. We will also offer more funds to local councils to set up expensive waste recycling facilities, with the aim that within the next fifteen years at least half of our city's waste will be recycled and put to good use.

(7) There is another incentive which I will use in the next five years if I have to. I think that if the general public do not prove that they can manage their own waste effectively, I will introduce a 'pay as you throw' metered home collection system. Basically, the more harmful to the environment your waste is, the more you will pay to have it removed. Also, if it's shown that you have not sorted your waste efficiently, you will pay more for it to be taken away. These are not measures that I want to introduce, but they will surely get the message across to those people who care little about what they throw away.

Source: Cambridge IGCSE E2L (paper 2) May/June 2006, page 8, Exercise 4

Paragraph	Section heading	Number of points
1		
2		
3		
4		
5		
6		
7		

Activity 13

Look at the text again. How many points can you find for each section heading in each paragraph? Complete the final column of the table in Activity **12**.

Activity 14

Here are the 11 main points from the text. Match them with the section headings: **a** *Problems associated with landfill sites*, **b** *Measures already in place to reduce problems on the sites*, **c** *Financial incentives to recycle waste*. Did you find the same number of points? If not, which ones didn't you find?

1 (more) funds to local councils

2 (unpleasant) smells

3 'pay as you throw' / metered home collection system

4 burying waste leads people to forget about it

5 lining of collection points / protective material

6 not pretty

7 risk of birth defects

8 tax reductions

9 landfill sites are filling up

10 toxic compounds entering groundwater (system)

11 use of deodoriser

C   Exam focus

You are going to look at some sample answers from IGCSE students to the following question:

Exercise 4

Read the article below about a gorilla named Koko, and then complete the notes.

Gorillas have a word for it

(1)   Koko is the first gorilla to have been taught sign language (a way of communicating by using hands and fingers rather than speech). With a vocabulary of more than 1000 words, she is the first to prove we share a world with other intelligent beings who feel emotions, look forward to celebrations and also have a sense of humour.

(2)   The 30-year study of Koko has redefined science's concept of gorilla intelligence. According to some scientists, genetically there is only a 2% difference between gorillas and humans: we share the same blood type, have the same number of hairs per square inch and also the same temperament. But what had not been recognised by the scientific community was that gorillas have the ability to learn a language and have complex emotions.

(3)   Koko lives in the Santa Cruz mountains in North America, in a wooded spot overlooking a valley. She has her own home, with curtains, and a nest of blankets, which is her bed, in one corner. She has a barrel on which she likes to sit when 'talking' to humans – gorillas feel more secure when they can look down on others – while her toys are spread everywhere. In addition she has an outside enclosure where she spends her days when it is not raining.

(4)   It is her conversations with her teacher, Dr Penny Patterson, that are inspiring. Penny explains: 'The reality of my discovery is that our abilities as humans, our skills, sensibilities and emotions are very similar to the great apes. What we have learnt is that gorillas are more complex than we ever imagined.'

(5)   When she began teaching Koko sign language, placing the little fingers of the one-year-old gorilla into the correct positions for 'drink', 'eat', 'more', and rewarding her with food, Dr Patterson had no idea how quickly Koko would learn. 'At first, it seemed Koko was using sign language as a tool to get something,' says Patterson. 'It became the kind of reward system that you could expect of a cat or a dog. But early in her training, she began to combine signs that made me think she was capable of more.' Now Koko is so proficient in sign language that if she doesn't know a word she invents one. For example, she didn't know the word for 'ring', so she combined the signs for 'finger' and 'bracelet' to express it.

(6)   Dr Patterson continues: 'Koko loves babies and young people. And when she is asked what gorillas like best, she always says "Gorilla love eat, good".' One of Patterson's favourite stories demonstrates Koko's sense of humour. When a visitor asked her to show him something scary, she held up a mirror to his face!

(7)   When Patterson asked her what she would like for her 11th birthday, Koko signed that she wanted a cat. The story of Koko's cat enabled Patterson to learn more about her student: the cat was hit by a car and Patterson had to break the news to Koko, who signed 'cry, sad, frown'. Then, once alone, Patterson heard Koko make the gorilla's distress call: a loud series of hoots.

(8)   From the age of three, Koko shared her accommodation with Michael who was intended as a mate. However, Michael died suddenly two years ago of a heart attack. 'Koko went into a depression following Michael's death,' says Patterson. 'She would sit for hours with her head hung low looking upset.'

(9)   Dr Patterson asked her if she was looking forward to moving to Hawaii, where Patterson is raising money to build a gorilla refuge. Koko signed 'Yes', provided she could have curtains in her new home!

Source: Cambridge IGCSE E2L (0510/02) Oct/Nov 2006, page 8, Exercise 4

Activity 15

Before you read the sample answers, read the section headings carefully:

a   Physical characteristics shared by gorillas and humans

b   Equipment used to furnish Koko's accommodation

c   How Koko was first taught sign language

d   Sad events in Koko's life

Activity 16

Now read the whole text. For each paragraph, decide what information is given for each of the section headings: **a**, **b**, **c** and **d**. How many points can you find for each section heading in each paragraph?

Paragraph	Section heading	Number of points
1		
2		
3		
4		
5		
6		
7		
8		
9		

Look at the three sample answers below from the Extended paper. Decide which are the best and worst answers, and say why.

(1)

Physical characteristics shared by gorillas and humans
- we have same number of hairs per inch
- same temperament and same blood type

Equipment used to furnish Koko's accommodation
- she had a bed
- she had curtains

How Koko was first taught sign language
- placing the little fingers into the correct position
- she combined the signs for finger and bracelet

Sad events in Koko's life
- cat was hit by a car
- Michael died suddenly of a heart attack

(2)

Physical characteristics shared by gorillas and humans
- same temperment
- gorillas have the ability to learn a language and have complex emotions

Equipment used to furnish Koko's accommodation
- toys are spread everywhere
- she has an outdoor enclosure
- a barel

How Koko was first taught sign language
- rewarding her with food
- at first, it seemed Koko was using sign language as a tool to get something

Sad events in Koko's life
- the cat was hitt by a car
- she would sit for hours with her head hung low looking upset

(3)

Physical characteristics shared by gorillas and humans
- share the same blood type
- same temperament

Equipment used to furnish Koko's accommodation
- curtains and a nest of blankets
- a barrel

How Koko was first taught sign language
- placing the little fingers into the correct position
- rewarding her with food

Sad events in Koko's life
- cat was hit by a car
- Michael died of a heart attack

Activity 18

Look at the examiners' comments for the three sample answers in Activity **17**. Match the answers (**1–3**) with the comments below (**a–c**). Give reasons for your choices.

a *The candidate was given seven marks out of a possible eight for the exercise.*

The candidate has answered in note form and has selected the correct information from the text. The second answer is incorrect as the candidate has not completely understood the wording of the section heading, which asks for **physical** *characteristics;* the same temperament *is a shared characteristic between gorillas and humans, but not a physical one. The candidate has given two correct points,* curtains and a nest of blankets *for the third answer. The candidate is only given one mark, however, because only the first idea is marked.*

b *The candidate was given five marks out of a possible eight for the exercise.*

The candidate has answered in note form. There are three mistakes, however. In the first answer the word square *has not been transferred and therefore the answer is not completely correct. Answer six is incorrect because* signs for finger and bracelet *is not* **how** *she was taught. The second answer cannot be given a mark because the first idea on the line is incorrect, even though it is followed by a good answer. It is important for candidates to take care when including more than one detail on the same line.*

c *The candidate was given three marks out of a possible eight for the exercise.*

The candidate has not always written in note form and some points have not been found. The answers are sometimes too long and are full sentences. In the second section, the candidate creates his/her own point in addition to those on the paper and cannot be given a mark, although the detail is correct. Only two answers are needed. In the first section, the candidate has not completely understood the section heading, which asks for **physical** *characteristics. There are other similar examples in the third and fourth sections. There are some spelling errors but the message is still clear and is accepted.*

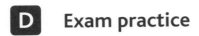

D · Exam practice

1 CORE

Exercise 4

Read the following article about an underwater clean-up campaign and then complete the notes on the opposite page.

Divers launch first underwater clean-up campaign

A group of divers from the Two Moon Diving Club (TMDC) has started the first clean-up campaign of its kind in Yemen – both underwater and on the beach! The clean-up campaign lasted for two full days on Kamaran Island in the Red Sea.

Five divers from Yemen and Egypt participated in the clean-up campaign, and despite the poor visibility underwater, they succeeded in collecting considerable amounts of garbage, including oil cans and rusty metal, from the water.

The first day of cleaning took place underwater as five scuba divers scoured a 500 metre squared area. Waste collected included plastic bags, pipes, shoes and ropes. The team managed to collect 40 kg of rubbish during its first dive. During the evening of the same day, divers continued clearing the underwater area, gathering another 10 kg of waste, much of it deposited by fishermen who do not stop to think about the terrible damage they are causing when they throw rubbish into the sea.

The next morning brought early heavy rain which destroyed some roads and made the ground very muddy and slippery. As a result, transportation on the island became extremely difficult for everyone. However, the team still managed to gather 17 students from the island as well as six villagers. With everybody ready, complete with T-shirts, gloves and collecting bags, they set off to clear the beaches.

The garbage collected was mostly non-organic materials that do not decompose, such as plastic bottles and bags. This is dangerous, as products such as these can kill many forms of marine life, including turtles. Plastic garbage also pollutes the bottom of the sea.

Chairman of the TMDC, Essam Al Sulaihi, said that a lack of understanding by the public, who simply throw their rubbish into the sea without thinking of the devastating impact that plastic bags and empty cans will have on the environment, is an enormous problem.

Adapted from 'Divers launch first underwater clean-up campaign', *Yemen Observer*, page 12, vol X1 issue 90, 15th November 2008

You are preparing to give a short talk to your diving club about TMDC's clean-up campaign. Prepare some notes to use as the basis for your talk.

Make **two** notes under each heading.

Problems faced by clean-up group

- _____
- _____

Rubbish collected underwater

- _____
- _____

Main causes of pollution

- _____
- _____

[Total: 6]

Exercise 4

Read the following article about taxis in Cairo, Egypt, and then complete the notes on the opposite page.

Cabs in Cairo

Little black taxis, often run-down and falling apart from decades of use, have for a long time been a prominent feature of Cairo's chaotic urban landscape. But their days may be numbered, thanks to a new taxi replacement programme aimed at phasing out older, potentially unsafe vehicles.

The government-sponsored initiative, launched earlier this year, allows drivers of taxis 20 years or older, mostly Fiats and Peugeots, to trade their cars for shiny new all-white ones at generous rates of financing. Drivers can choose between five different locally manufactured car models.

According to officials, more than 11,000 brand new taxis, sporting trademark checked stripes on the sides, have already hit the streets of the capital, and they've been welcomed enthusiastically by passengers. Many people say that not only are the new taxis more comfortable, but they also make the streets of Cairo far more presentable. Furthermore, taxi fares have only increased by a small amount.

The poor condition of most vintage black and white taxis is almost legendary. Passengers often have to deal with windows and doors that do not open and close, and heavy, thick petrol fumes. Air conditioning is unheard of. The new all-white taxis, meanwhile, are cleaner, more fuel-efficient and provide air conditioning on request. Furthermore, all the new taxis come equipped with functioning fare meters, which avoids arguments and sometimes fights with passengers!

The government hopes to replace all of the capital's 40,000 elderly black cabs soon, but not everyone in Cairo will be happy to see them go. Hotel manager Ibrahim Al-Toukhy says that the old black cabs were rickety and run-down, and maybe even a little dangerous, but they were part of the city, and part of Cairo's character.

Adapted from 'Cairo's new cabs', *Gulf Life*, Gulf Air in-flight magazine, page 51, October 2009

You are preparing to give a short talk to some students about taxis in Cairo. Prepare some notes to use as the basis for your talk.

Problems with older Cairo taxis

- _____
- _____
- _____
- _____

Advantages of new taxis for passengers

- _____
- _____
- _____
- _____

[Total: 8]

Exercise 4

Read the following article about the new sport of parkour, and then complete the notes on the opposite page.

A building is not an obstacle

A new urban sport, parkour, is hitting the streets. It has evolved from obstacle course training into a fitness option for young people. In parkour, the outside world is the gym! The bridges, buildings and railings of each and every city are the equipment. The goal of parkour is a direct route from one place to another. You meet an obstacle, you overcome it.

Mark Toorock, who teaches the techniques of parkour at his fitness gym, says that parkour is a method to train the body and mind using obstacles as the medium. He says that this new sport is demanding and takes years to master, and beginners should realise that they will not be jumping over buildings and walls any time soon!

But Toorock, who used to be a martial arts expert, says that everyone can benefit from learning the basic skills involved in parkour like running, jumping and crawling. These are the things that humans used to have to do all the time, but today, because of modern transport methods, these basic skills are no longer used on a regular basis. The original idea of parkour was to return to running and jumping as basic elements in moving from one place to another.

Georges Hebert, a French navy officer, was so impressed by the effortless athleticism of African tribes that he devised a training method based on running, climbing, jumping, balancing and throwing. The word *parkour* comes from *parcours de combatant*, the French term for a military obstacle course. The French word for people who participate in the sport is *traceurs* or *traceuses*, meaning 'people who go fast'.

Dr Kenneth Kao has been a *traceur* since college. He says that *traceurs* are some of the fittest and most neurologically coordinated people he has ever met. The basic parkour techniques of crawling, running, rolling and jumping were ingrained into our body movements at a very early age. Every action in parkour is natural, so each *traceur* must have the ability to move in this way.

Dr Kao explains that the sport of parkour is not extreme – it is the environment which is extreme and dangerous. Being outside, jumping off railings and flipping over park benches can be quite frightening, so parkour courses in gyms concentrate on practising all the individual moves to make everything easier. Gyms provide thick floor matting for rolling and rubberised boxes for jumping over. However, that is not real parkour because it's indoors with a fixed obstacle. The goal for everyone is to go outdoors.

Adapted from 'In parkour, city is gym', *Arab News*, page 16, Saudi Arabia, 7th October 2009

You are preparing to give a short talk to some students about the new sport of parkour. Prepare some notes to use as the basis for your talk.

Background and development of parkour

- _____

- _____

- _____

Personal and physical qualities required for parkour

- _____

- _____

- _____

Parkour in the gym

- _____

- _____

[Total: 8]

Exercise 4

Read the following article about shopping for people with a food allergy or intolerance, and then complete the notes on the opposite page.

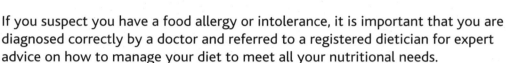

Shopping for sufferers of a food allergy or intolerance

If you suspect you have a food allergy or intolerance, it is important that you are diagnosed correctly by a doctor and referred to a registered dietician for expert advice on how to manage your diet to meet all your nutritional needs.

What is a food allergy?

Food allergies involve the body's immune system. The body reacts to certain allergens in food by producing antibodies, which can cause immediate and severe symptoms such as swollen lips or eyes, vomiting, skin rashes, and, in the most extreme cases, difficulty breathing and a severe fall in blood pressure (anaphylactic shock).

What is food intolerance?

This does not normally involve the immune system, and symptoms may not be as immediate or severe as in food allergies. Symptoms may include headache, fatigue and digestive problems. An example is lactose intolerance, when certain people cannot digest the sugar in milk. Food intolerance is harder to diagnose than allergy. The only reliable way to diagnose it is to cut out the suspected food from the diet to see if the symptoms get better. If the symptoms improve, the food should be reintroduced and monitored for signs of the symptoms returning. This process should only take place under the supervision of a registered dietician.

Tips for food shopping and storage

If you have a diagnosed allergy or food intolerance, it's essential you take care to avoid cross-contamination with the allergen. When you buy or cook food for someone with a food allergy, you will need to check the ingredients to ensure the product does not contain the allergen (for example nuts, wheat, milk) that the person is allergic to. Also, make sure you store foods such as nuts, peanuts, flour and milk separately in closed containers in order to avoid cross-contamination. Furthermore, always wash your hands thoroughly with hot water and soap and avoid touching other foods until you have finished preparing the meal. Make sure all cooking equipment is washed properly, and this includes work surfaces, chopping boards, mixing bowls, pans, cake tins, knives and utensils. Finally ... never use oil that has previously been cooked in.

Adapted from 'Allergy – making sense of food allergy and intolerance', leaflet produced by Sainsbury's Supermarkets Ltd, www.sainsburys.co.uk

You are preparing to give a short talk to some students about shopping for a food allergy or intolerance. Prepare some notes to use as the basis for your talk.

Body's reaction to food allergies

- _____

- _____

- _____

How to diagnose food intolerance

- _____

- _____

Things to remember when cooking

- _____

- _____

- _____

[Total: 8]

Exercise 5

In this unit you will learn about Exercise 5, the summary-writing exercise in the IGCSE E2L examination, and practise the skills you need.

 ## Introduction

What is Exercise 5?

Exercise 5 in both the Core and Extended papers is a summary-writing activity. In the Core paper you use your notes from Exercise 4 to help you write your summary; in the Extended paper you have to read a different text to summarise.

Exercise 5

Read the following research into people's effect on dolphins. **Write a summary of what the 'swim-with-dolphins' tourist industry should be doing to minimise the effect on dolphins.**

Your summary should be about 100 words (and no longer than 120 words). You should use your own words as far as possible.

You will receive up to 6 marks for the content of your summary and up to 4 marks for the style and accuracy of your language.

Research has shown that while dolphins can move away if they do not want to interact with human swimmers, they do not like it at all if the swimmers slip into the water directly on top of them or if humans are in their path of travel. However, if swimmers enter the water to one side of them, the dolphins do not avoid the swimmers to the same extent. This possibly seems like less threatening behaviour to them.

In all cases, the dolphins seem to have become more sensitised to the presence of the swimmers. For dolphins, swimming amongst or with humans is not necessarily a high priority. This research has shown that only 19% of any group of dolphins will participate in interaction. Young dolphins are the most likely to interact; they do seem curious about being with humans. It is believed that they see humans as 'entertainment' and that the interaction is a new and unusual experience for them ...

Source: Cambridge IGCSE E2L (0510/22) May/June 2008, pages 10–11, Exercise 5 (Extended)

How many marks are there?

In the Core paper there are four marks for this exercise, all for language (writing), while in the Extended paper there are ten: six for content (reading) and four for language (writing).

What are the assessment objectives?

Because in the Core paper there is no text in Exercise 5, there are no reading assessment objectives. However, in both papers, for writing, you are assessed on your ability to:

- communicate clearly, accurately and appropriately (Writing assessment objective 1)
- convey information and express opinions effectively (W2)
- employ and control a variety of grammatical structures (W3)
- demonstrate knowledge and understanding of a range of appropriate structures (W4)
- observe conventions of paragraphing, punctuation and spelling (W5).

Check!

What do you think these words and phrases mean?

- communicate appropriately _____
- convey information _____
- employ and control _____
- a range of appropriate structures _____
- observe conventions _____

In the Extended paper, you are also assessed on your ability to:

- understand and respond to information presented in a variety of forms (R1)
- select and organise material relevant to specific purposes (R2)
- recognise, understand and distinguish between facts, ideas and opinions (R3).

What does Exercise 5 look like?

In the Core paper, Exercise 5 is linked to Exercise 4. The instructions for Exercise 5 come immediately after the note-making form. There are lines for you to write your summary on. In the Extended paper, you will see a text on the left-hand page, and a page of lines on the right-hand page for you to write your summary on.

What's the difference between the Core and Extended papers?

Check!

Complete the information in the box with the words and phrases below.

Exercise 5   summary   the notes   Exercise 4   Extended paper   text   is linked

> The main difference between the two papers is that in the Core paper, Exercise 5
> _____ to Exercise 4. This means that you can make use of
> _____ you made in _____ to write a
> 70-word summary in _____ . For the _____,
> you need to read another_____ and write a _____ of
> up to 100 words from it.

What do I have to do?

The focus for Exercise 5 is summary writing. Remember that in the Core paper there is no text to read – you can use your notes from Exercise 4 as the basis for your summary.

The question explains what you have to do:

> Look at your notes in Exercise 4 above. Using the ideas in your notes, write a summary of the recent research into the performance of top sports stars.
>
> Source: Cambridge IGCSE E2L (paper 12) May/June 2009, page 9, Exercise 5

Remember to use your own words as far as possible. In the Core paper you need to write 70 words.

Remember!

- There is no text to read in the Core paper – use your notes from Exercise 4.
- Use headings in your notes to order the ideas in your summary.
- Write no more than 70 words for the Core paper.
- Use your own words as far as possible.

In the Extended paper the question explains what the text is about.

For example:

> Read the following article about young people and television.

It also explains what you have to do:

> Write a summary on the opposite page of the negative effects on children who watch too much television.
>
> Source: Cambridge IGCSE E2L (paper 21) May/June 2009, page 10, Exercise 5

You need to find the information in the text and use it to write a summary. Use your own words as far as possible and write about 100 words (and no more than 120 words) in total. Remember that there are up to six marks for the content of your summary and up to four marks for the style and accuracy of your language.

Remember!

- For the Extended paper, carefully read and underline parts of the question before reading the text.
- Write about 100 words (no more than 120 words) for the Extended paper.
- If you write more than 120 words, the extra words will **not** be marked.
- There is usually no need to summarise the whole text.

What do I need to know?

In the Core paper, you do not need to re-read the text in Exercise 4. All you need to do is write in sentence form the information from your notes in Exercise 4. You may look at the text again, but it should not be necessary and it can waste time. Use the space provided to guide you when writing the summary. If your summary is longer than the number of answer lines, you have probably written too much.

In the Extended paper, you need to read a new text and identify the main points which you then transfer into your summary. Study the question very carefully first to find out exactly what you have to do. It is a good idea to underline the different parts of the question before you read the text. This will help you to decide which parts of the text answer the different parts of the question. Remember that you do **not** usually need to summarise the whole text.

What else do I need to know?

- The summary should be about 100 words (and no more than 120 words). The examiner will not mark anything after 120 words.
- If you do not use your own words, you will not be given more than two marks for language. Try to use different words and expressions which have the same meaning as those in the text.
- Sometimes the task involves writing about **two** aspects (parts) of the text. Use suitable connecting words and phrases.
- If there are two aspects to the summary, you must try to find points from both areas. Full marks cannot be given if you do not try to answer both parts of the question.

Here are the descriptors for marking the language in Exercise 5 (Core and Extended level descriptors are almost identical). Match each one with a mark: 0 (lowest), 1, 2, 3 or 4 (highest).

Descriptors	Marks
Expression good, with attempts to group and sequence ideas in own words.	
Expression limited OR reliance on copying out the notes, but some sense of order.	
Meaning obscure because of density of language errors and serious problems with expression OR nothing of relevance.	
Expression very good: clear, orderly grouping and sequencing, largely own words.	
Expression weak OR reliance on lifting from the passage.	

Source: Cambridge IGCSE E2L Mark scheme for the May/June 2009 question paper 0510/11

Note: This information is from a 2009 mark scheme as stated above. Mark schemes for other sessions may vary slightly.

B Preparation

Understanding the question

Look at this question from an Extended IGCSE examination paper:

> Read the following article about Romina, the gorilla. **Write a summary on the opposite page describing how her behaviour has changed since her eye operation.**
>
> **Your summary should be about 100 words (and no more than 120 words). You should use your own words as far as possible.**
>
> You will be given up to 6 marks for the content of your summary and up to 4 marks for the style and accuracy of your language.

Source: Cambridge IGCSE E2L (0510/02) May/June 2006, page 10, Exercise 5

What are the **three** most important pieces of information in this question?

_____

_____

_____

Surgeons restore sight to shy gorilla

A bullied gorilla is finally able to stand up for herself after an eye surgeon operated on a cataract condition that had left her virtually blind from birth.

Romina's sudden ability to see came as a shock to other gorillas at Bristol Zoo, England. She chased off another gorilla who had become used to stealing her food, and is also showing interest in a possible mate. Romina and Bongo, her potential mate, arrived at Bristol from Rome Zoo as part of an international breeding programme to help the threatened species. Her vision had been an impenetrable mist; unable to see farther than a few inches, she had to feel her way around.

The operation on the 21-year-old gorilla was carried out by Jenny Watts, an opthalmologist. She said, 'Her eyes are completely black, but otherwise she was no different to a human patient, apart from the pungent smell of gorilla, which was like nothing I had ever smelt before.'

For the operation, the 120 kg gorilla was first shot with a tranquilliser gun, then taken for surgery at the University of Bristol veterinary school. Sharon Redrobe, the chief vet at the zoo said, 'We had to tranquillise her before putting her in the back of the van because gorillas can be dangerous and are easily strong enough to kill a human. And, of course, you can't explain to her what is happening.'

There was an immediate transformation in her behaviour after regaining consciousness following the operation. Ms Redrobe said, 'We could tell she could see straight away. She immediately reached towards food without having to feel her way. The other day, one of our other gorillas, Salome, tried to run off with Romina's banana and was chased the length of the gorilla enclosure. Salome had the shock of her life.' Ms Redrobe added, 'Salome used to hit her over the head and Romina wouldn't know what was happening. Salome used to steal Romina's food.'

The zoo's gorilla-keeper had to persuade Romina to accept antibiotic eye drops four times a day for a week before the operation and for two weeks afterwards. Only their close bond made it possible to deliver the drops which stopped the eye becoming infected. Before the operation she would hardly go outside. Now she interacts with the other gorillas in ways which she didn't do before and she loves exploring the gorilla island, which was not possible previously. Her life has been improved in just about every way. Jo Gipps, the director of Bristol Zoo, said that lowland gorillas were seriously threatened in their native habitat in forests of Central and Western Africa. Although there are estimated to be about 90,000 of the animals left in the wild, they are being hunted for meat as well as being chased out of their habitat by logging.

Until her operation, Romina showed little interest in Bongo, but she has now been observed play-fighting with her potential mate. They had been together for 18 years and had developed a close relationship. What happens next may be dependent on whether she likes what she sees.

Source: Cambridge IGCSE E2L (0510/02) May/June 2006, page 10, Exercise 5

Activity 2

What information does this phrase give you? What do you know **before** you read the text?

... her behaviour has changed since her eye operation ...

Activity 3

Based on your answer to Activity **2**, what information do you need to look for in the text?

Finding important information in the text

Activity 4

Quickly skim read paragraphs 1–4 of the text *Surgeons restore sight to shy gorilla* on page **87**. Which of the paragraphs will help you to write your summary? Which will not?

Activity 5

Now look at paragraphs 5–7. Which of the paragraphs will help you to write your summary? Which will not?

Activity 6

Look at the following information about how Romina's behaviour has changed since her eye operation. Decide in which paragraph each piece of information can be found. Underline the information in the text.

- able to reach for food
- can stand up for herself
- chased off another gorilla (Salome) who was stealing food
- doesn't have to feel her way around
- explores
- interacts, communicates with other gorillas
- now able to go outside
- plays with Bongo
- shows interest in and play-fights with a possible mate

Activity 7

There are **nine** pieces of information in the list in Activity **6**. However, **two** pieces of information are repeated. Which two?

_____

_____

Putting it all together

Activity 8

When you have found all the important points from the text, you need to think about how to put it all together into a good summary. Which words can help you to link ideas? Make two lists in the table below.

Sequence words	Other words
Firstly	However

Activity 9

Remember that a summary is **not** a composition, so you do not need to write an introduction or a conclusion. However, it may help you to get started if you include a very short introductory sentence. Look again at the exam question in Activity **1**. What information does the question ask you to find? Use this information to begin your summary.

Romina's behaviour ...

_____

_____

_____

Activity 10

Now, using the notes from Activity **6**, your introductory phrase from Activity **9** and some of your linking words from Activity **8**, write your summary. Remember to keep to the word count.

_____

_____

_____

_____

_____

_____

_____

_____

_____

_____

_____

_____

C Exam focus

EXTENDED

You are going to look at some sample answers from IGCSE students to an Exercise 5 question.

Activity 11

Before you read the text and sample answers, read the question at the top of page **91** carefully. What exactly is your summary going to be about?

_____

_____

Read the following research into people's effect on dolphins. **On the opposite page, write a summary of what the 'swim-with-dolphins' tourist industry should be doing to minimise the effect on dolphins.**

Your summary should be about 100 words (and no more than 120 words). You should use your own words as far as possible.

You will receive up to 6 marks for the content of your summary and up to 4 marks for the style and accuracy of your language.

Dolphins

(1) Humans have always been fascinated by dolphins and there has been a long history of association between the two. Over time this has turned into a rapidly expanding worldwide tourist activity – swimming with dolphins. The chance to see dolphins in the wild is often a lifetime dream for many people, but few consider the implications of actually swimming with these animals.

(2) The 'swim-with-dolphins' tourist industry is becoming more popular every year and tour operators are always on the lookout to give their tourist swimmers the best experience they can. After all, it can cost a large amount of money to have this kind of holiday experience. So tour operators try to place eager swimmers as near as possible to the dolphins by trying to predict where the dolphins will be. The swimmers usually enter the water from the back of a stationary boat and swim freely in the water.

(3) Research has shown that while dolphins can move away if they do not want to interact with human swimmers, they do not like it at all if the swimmers slip into the water directly on top of them or if humans are in their path of travel. However, if swimmers enter the water to one side of them, the dolphins do not avoid the swimmers to the same extent. This possibly seems like less threatening behaviour to them.

(4) In all cases, the dolphins seem to have become more sensitised to the presence of the swimmers. For dolphins, swimming amongst or with humans is not necessarily a high priority. This research has shown that only 19% of any group of dolphins will participate in interaction. Young dolphins are the most likely to interact; they do seem curious about being with humans. It is believed that they see humans as 'entertainment' and that the interaction is a new and unusual experience for them.

(5) It is frequently asked whether 'swim-with-dolphins' tourism should be discontinued. The advice is that dolphins should be given substantial periods of time throughout the day when they are not exposed to tourism. Permitted interactions should not be too intrusive to the dolphins since there could be mothers and calves present in dolphin groups. There should also be educational campaigns about the creatures and the likely threats to them. If not, in the long term there could be detrimental effects on the dolphins' well-being which may not become evident until many years later.

(6) It is not easy to explain to someone that they cannot fulfil their lifelong dreams because the dolphins are resting, or that a mother dolphin and calf are in the area. But if we are to enjoy these remarkable animals and not just use them for our entertainment, then we must carefully monitor the 'swim-with-dolphins' industry worldwide.

Source: Cambridge IGCSE E2L (0510/22) May/June 2008, pages 10–11, Exercise 5

Activity 12

Now read the text on page **91**. For each paragraph, decide what the main topic is.

Example:

Paragraph 1 – talks about the history of humans and dolphins

_____

Paragraph 2 –_____

_____

Paragraph 3 –_____

_____

Paragraph 4 –_____

_____

Paragraph 5 –_____

_____

Paragraph 6 –_____

_____

Activity 13

Compare your ideas above with the list given here.

Paragraph 1 – talks about the history of humans and dolphins

Paragraph 2 – the popularity of 'swim-with-dolphins'

Paragraph 3 – threats to dolphins

Paragraph 4 – young dolphins

Paragraph 5 – negative impact of tourism

Paragraph 6 – dolphins are not just for entertainment

Activity 14

Which of the six paragraphs do **not** contain any information relevant to the summary question?

_____

Activity 15

Look at the three sample answers on page **93**. Decide which are the best and worst answers, and say why. Think about both content **and** language.

(1) The 'swim-with-dolphins' industry is becoming more popular every year. Tour operators try to place swimmers as near as possible to the dolphins. But certain rules should be followed to minimise the effects on these creatures.

Firstly, swimmers should not enter the water directly above the dolphins or in their pathways. They should get into the water to one side of the dolphins. Moreover, dolphins should have long periods of time during the day when they can rest. This is particularly important when dolphin groups contain mothers and calves.

Finally, there should be more information about these creatures and the threats that humans bring through educational campaigns. We must continue to monitor the 'swim-with-dolphins' industry worldwide.

(2) Human friends animal dolphins

The swim-with-dolphins tourist is large and popular industry They swiming near of dolphins to predict where dolphins will go. The swimer should enter the water from side of dolphin and swim freely in water. The dolphins go away if they donot want to interact with human. swimer. if they enter one side the dolphins will swimer to the same extent. They have threatening behaviour. nineteen percentage of dolphins participate interaction. Human is for them entertainment and it is new and unusual experience The day they are not expose to tourist. The long fulfil dream because dolphins are resting and interactions not be too intrusive since there could be mothers and calves present.

(3) The 'swim with dolphin' industry is a very entertaining thing to go on by we have to consider the effect on the dolphins.

Firstly, the industry should be monitored and the program should come up at least once in two years. Dolphin have also become sensiticed to the presence of swimmers. And dolphin do not like it at all when swimmers slip into the water directly on top of them or if humans are in their travel pathway.

Secondly, dolphins should be given their own rest time, so they are not exposed to tourism the whole while. There should also be educational campaigns about the creatures and the likely threats to them.

Activity 16

Look at the examiners' comments for the three sample answers in Activity **15**. Match the answers (**1–3**) with the comments below (**a–c**). Give reasons for your choices.

a Content

The candidate has found all the main points from the text and has written them in a clear and understandable way. The first two sentences introduce the topic and then the candidate focuses on selecting the main points. The final sentence finishes the summary well. The candidate was given a maximum six marks for content.

Language

The expression is very good throughout the piece. The language is perfect for a summary and there are very few unnecessary words or expressions. The language is focused and there is good use of linking words so the piece flows well. The candidate copies some expressions from the text but has used own words wherever possible. There are no mistakes of grammar or punctuation and the candidate was given the maximum four marks for language.

b Content

The candidate stays on the topic throughout but language mistakes cause problems. The summary is really just disconnected ideas, although the first sentence tries to introduce the topic. The candidate was given two marks out of a possible six for content.

Language

There are many serious grammar and spelling mistakes – at times the meaning is unclear. There are some clearer expressions where the message can be understood, but in general the language is weak. The candidate tries to use own words but with little success. The candidate was given one mark out of a possible four for language.

c Content

The candidate identifies some of the main points towards the end of the summary, but the first part does not answer the question. In the first sentence, the candidate tries to make a good introduction but then does not identify or express the main points until the second half of the summary. The candidate was given four marks out of six for content.

Language

The candidate does not use a variety of expression, especially in the first sentences, although the language does improve later in the summary. There is some sense of order and the candidate uses firstly *and* secondly *well. The reader can generally understand the meaning. There is some copying from the text, however, and when the candidate tries to use own words and expressions, there are several grammar mistakes. The candidate was given two marks out of a possible four for language.*

You are going to answer an Exercise 5 question and look at some sample answers to it from other IGCSE students. The Exercise 5 question, which is at the bottom of this page, uses notes from the Exercise 4 question above it:

Exercise 4

You are preparing to give a short talk to your hill-walking group about Jake Meyer. Prepare some notes to use as the basis of your talk.

Make **two** notes under each heading.

Jake's achievements

- youngest Briton to stand on Everest's summit
- ....
- ....

Jake's training details

- relies on feeling good and his youth
- ....
- ....

Dangers encountered on his latest challenge

- ....
- ....

[Total: 6]

Exercise 5

Imagine you have given your talk to the group. You want to produce a written summary to remind them of the details of the talk.

Look at your notes in Exercise 4. Using the ideas in your notes, write a summary of Jake Meyer's mountaineering challenges.

Your summary should be one paragraph of no more than 70 words. You should use your own words as far as possible.

Source: Cambridge IGCSE E2L (0510/12) May/June 2008, page 9, Exercise 5

Here are your Exercise 4 notes:

Jake's achievements
- youngest Briton to stand on Everest's summit
- youngest man to climb seven summits
- speed record achieved

Jake's training details
- relies on feeling good and his youth
- keeps going without stopping
- ignores pain

Dangers encountered on his latest challenge
- altitude
- road accidents

Remember that in the Core paper Exercise 5 is marked for **language**, not **content**.

Activity 17

Use these Exercise 4 notes to write your Exercise 5 summary. Begin like this:

Jake Meyer has faced several mountaineering challenges ...

_____

_____

_____

_____

_____

_____

_____

[Total: 4]

Activity 18

Look at the three sample answers below. Decide which are the best and worst answers, and say why. Think about the **language**.

1. Jake holds the world record in climbing mountains at the time. He already reached Mount Everest faster than anybody else did. He often has to face dangers on his challenges for example by bears or snakes which are usual in some of the areas. Jake has also already climbed all of the highest peaks in the 48 states of America. His next challenge is hopefully all the European peaks.

(2) Jake Meyer was the youngest man to climb 7 sumits and he achieved the speed record. Jake says that he keeps on going so that the pain will subside and it isn't about the speed. He faced not only the dangers of alitude but the very real threat of attack by bears and snakes, and, in driving from coast to coast, the worry of road accidents.

(3) Its for the people who are climbing mountain: when you want to climb a mountain you have to be strong don't be lazy. You have to achieve your aim that you are aiming. You don't have to be stopping all the time, try your best to do it without sitting and getting tired all the time. don't ever be scared of corse you will do it.

Activity 19

Look at the examiners' comments for the three sample answers in Activity **18**. Match the answers (**1–3**) with the comments below (**a–c**). Give reasons for your choices.

a *The candidate has followed the word limit but there is a lot of copying from the text. There are a few spelling mistakes and mixing of past and present tenses. There is, however, a sense of order and the candidate was given two marks out of a possible four for language. In order to get three marks the candidate needed to make more of an attempt to use his/her own words.*

---

b *The candidate has followed the word limit but much of the language is repeated and does not show much variety. There are several basic punctuation and grammar mistakes, and little sense of order. The message is also too general. The candidate was given one mark out of a possible four for language. In order to get higher marks, the candidate needed to focus more on the headings in the notes to order the ideas better.*

---

c *The candidate has followed the word limit and the spelling and punctuation are correct although there is some mixing of the past and present tenses. The expressions are good and the candidate has tried to order the ideas correctly. The candidate was given three marks out of a possible four for language. In order to get four marks the candidate needed to show more variety – for example, through the use of linking words.*

See opposite page for Exam practice section

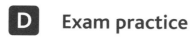 **Exam practice**

1 CORE

Look back at the first text in Section **D** of the Exercise 4 unit. Remember that in the Core exam Exercises 4 and 5 are linked.

Exercise 5

Imagine you have given your talk to your diving club. You want to produce a written summary to remind them of the details of the talk.

Look at your notes in Exercise 4. Using the ideas in your notes, write a summary of the main points.

Your summary should be one paragraph of no more than 70 words. You should use your own words as far as possible.

_____

_____

_____

_____

_____

_____

_____

_____

[Total: 4]

Exercise 5

Read the following text about exploring Jordan. **On the opposite page, write a summary of the activities that Jordan offers tourists.**

Your summary should be about 100 words (and no more than 120 words). You should use your own words as far as possible.

You will receive up to 6 marks for the content of your summary and up to 4 marks for the style and accuracy of your language.

Explore Jordan

Wadi Rum is the name given to a valley cut into the sandstone and granite rock in southwest Jordan. It is the largest wadi (riverbed) in Jordan. The name Rum most likely comes from an Aramaic word meaning 'high' or 'elevated'. The area around Wadi Rum is now also one of Jordan's most important tourist destinations, and attracts an increasing number of foreign tourists, particularly trekkers, but also for camel safaris or simply day-trippers from Aqaba or Petra. In contrast, there are almost no local or Arab tourists, though nearby Disi attracts young people from Amman at the weekends.

Popular activities in the desert environment include camping under the stars, riding Arab horses, and rock-climbing amongst the massive rock formations. Jebal Rum (*jebal* means 'mountain') is 1,574 metres above sea level and is the second highest peak in Jordan, rising directly above the Rum valley opposite Jebal um Ishrin.

But Jordan is not simply a desert environment – it also contains the area which is the lowest point on the face of the Earth – the incredible Dead Sea, popular with tourists for swimming. This vast stretch of water receives a number of incoming rivers, including the River Jordan. Once the waters reach the Dead Sea they are landlocked and have nowhere to go, so they evaporate, leaving behind a dense, rich cocktail of salts and minerals that supply industry, agriculture and medicine with some of its finest products. Once again, tourists benefit and can participate in water spa treatments and water therapies.

The Dead Sea is located in the Syro-African Rift, a 4,000-mile fault line in the Earth's crust. The lowest point of dry land on Earth is the shoreline of the Dead Sea at 1,300 feet below sea level. Because the lake is at the lowest point, this means that water does not drain from it. Every day, seven million tons of water evaporate from the lake, but the minerals remain, causing the salt content to increase. Figures for the Dead Sea's salinity today range from 25% to 35%.

But the greatest tourist attraction is the incredible city of Petra. It is without doubt Jordan's most valuable treasure. It is a vast, unique city, carved into the sheer rock face by the Nabataeans, an industrious Arab people who settled here more than 2,000 years ago, turning it into an important junction for the silk, spice and other trade routes that linked China, India and southern Arabia with Egypt, Syria, Greece and Rome. Today, visitors can marvel at the architecture and explore life as it was thousands of years ago.

Adapted from Le Meridien Hotels and Resorts in-house magazine, page 13, October 2009, www.lemeridien.com

[Total: 10]

Exercise 5

Read the following text about the first Arab to reach the North Magnetic Pole. **On the opposite page, write a summary of the problems Nabil al Busaidi faced on his journey.**

Your summary should be about 100 words (and no more than 120 words). You should use your own words as far as possible.

You will receive up to 6 marks for the content of your summary and up to 4 marks for the style and accuracy of your language.

First Arab to the North Pole

The Arctic is not a safe place to be by any stretch of the imagination. Essentially a vast, floating block of ice, with only a handful of tiny landmasses, the landscape can be almost totally different from year to year. Even the most experienced explorers are lucky to return with all their fingers and toes, not to mention their lives.

Into this hostile environment stepped Nabil al Busaidi. In fact, he didn't just step – he stepped and skied his way across 650 km, pulling 50 kg of equipment. He also carried the flag of the Sultanate of Oman, which he held aloft at the North Magnetic Pole, becoming the first Arab to achieve this impressive feat.

On the way to the Pole, Nabil was driven by the reward of success and the pain at the thought of failure. 'On the final day, what kept me going was being the first to get to the Pole. When I was desperate to fall asleep, that's what kept me going. I kept on thinking, *I'm going to make history, straighten your back, get a grip on yourself and don't mess this up.*

Throughout the 20-whatever days, every minute there was a different thing that kept me going, either the fear of failure, the fear of dying or the reward of finishing and getting somewhere warm.'

His exhaustion was often so absolute that vivid hallucinations plagued his progress. The ever-present cold, averaging around −40 °C but dropping as low as a recorded −81 °C, is his overriding memory of the experience. As an Omani, Nabil had an additional 30 °C drop in temperature to get used to, compared to his British teammates.

Apart from the extreme cold, polar bears were a common feature of the journey, and Nabil and the team had their fair share of bear encounters. 'Polar bears are dangerous, but they are not that threatening because they don't intend to harm humans. They're usually either curious or just don't care. We saw five bears, and none were aggressive. Two just walked through the camp and ignored us. One was looking through our things in the tent; another came and ripped the tent open, but the girl who was inside hit the bear on the nose with a saucepan. It walked away looking rather unhappy!' says Nabil.

One final problem was the strain put on team relations by the severity of the conditions, especially during the first three stages of the journey. However, during the fourth and final leg, the team worked so well together that they travelled 130 km in only two and a half days.

Adapted from 'Mission accomplished', *The Week*, pages 1–4, 13 May 2009, published by Apex Press and Publishing, Sultanate of Oman, www.theweek.co.om

_____

_____

_____

_____

_____

_____

_____

_____

_____

_____

_____

_____

_____

_____

[Total: 10]

Exercise 5

Read the following text about exam preparation. **On the opposite page, write a summary of the advice given on how to study before an exam.**

Your summary should be about 100 words (and no more than 120 words). You should use your own words as far as possible.

You will receive up to 6 marks for the content of your summary and up to 4 marks for the style and accuracy of your language.

Exam success

Being successful in an exam is not just about studying hard and knowing the subject inside out. There are a few other things that you can do that will help ensure you get the grades you need.

Research has shown that the calmer the mind, the better its capability to register and retrieve information. Every time you sit down to study, give yourself five minutes to calm your mind. When the mind is relaxed, it is in the 'state of alpha', where your brain waves are at about seven to fourteen cycles per second, the most conducive state for studying.

Choose a quiet place for studying and have everything handy that you need: books, pens, something to drink. Relax your body and mind and visualise the day of the results, and see yourself being congratulated by your family, friends and teachers. Enjoy the experience. And now you should be completely charged up and ready to absorb and retain important information.

Depending on what you want to study, and how much you have to cover, plan your time carefully. It's a good idea to make a list of all the important things you have to learn, in order of importance, and estimate how much time you need for each one. Add it all up and compare this with how much time you have available. This will tell you if you have time to read slowly and carefully, or if you can only skim read; also, it will show you how many times you can afford to look over the same information, and how to pace yourself so that you can get everything done. Allocate time for studying, revising and relaxing, and try to take a break for about two minutes after every twenty minutes of studying.

Because stress can have a negative effect on your memory, it's important to stay calm during tests. While that's easier said than done, there are several stress relief techniques that can help to calm you down whenever you feel overwhelmed. Breathing exercises during the examination, for example, can be extremely effective in helping you relax and reverse your stress response: just take deep breaths, and let the stress come out when you exhale. Remember also that not getting enough sleep before the examination can cause problems, as can not eating properly, so ensure that you sleep and eat well before a test.

Adapted from 'Be calm for your exams', *The Gulf Today*, page 39, 28th February 2008

[Total: 10]

Exercises 6 and 7

In this unit you will learn about Exercises 6 and 7, the writing exercises in the IGCSE E2L examination, and practise the skills you need.

 A ## Introduction

What are Exercises 6 and 7?

Exercises 6 and 7 in both the Core and Extended papers are longer writing activities. You need to produce a piece of writing in response to a short prompt on the question paper. The two questions will ask you to produce different types of writing: Exercise 6 might ask you to write an informal letter to a friend describing a visit to the cinema, for example, while Exercise 7 might ask you to write a formal article for a school newspaper arguing about the effects of smoking. For each question you will be given information on the **purpose**, **format** and **audience** for your writing.

Check!

a What do you think these words mean?
- purpose
- format
- audience

b Identify and underline the purpose, format and audience in the **two** examination questions on the page opposite.

c What other important information is given to you in the questions? Find at least **three** things in each question.

_____

_____

_____

_____

_____

_____

Exercise 6

You school is starting its own monthly magazine and students have been invited to write for it.

Write a letter to the magazine editor telling him or her why you want to be involved.

In your letter you should:

- include information about yourself and your writing skills
- say why you want to write for the magazine
- say what your interests are and what you could write about.

Your letter should be between 150 and 200 words long. Do not write an address.

You will receive up to 9 marks for the content of your letter, and up to 9 marks for the style and accuracy of your language.

CORE

Exercise 7

Your school is planning a careers day and is going to invite people from the local community to talk about their jobs.

Here are some comments from students in your school about careers:

'I think this is a great opportunity – we can think about which university course to study.'

'I think real work experience would be more useful than listening to people just talking about work.'

'I have no idea what I want to do in the future – the careers day should give me some ideas.'

'I can't see any point in the careers day – there are very few jobs around here.'

As a member of the student council you have been asked to write an article for your school magazine giving your ideas about the careers day.

Your article should be between 100 and 150 words long.

The comments above may give you some ideas but you are free to use any ideas of your own.

You will receive up to 5 marks for the content of your article, and up to 5 marks for the style and accuracy of your language.

How many marks are there?

There are a lot of marks available for Exercises 6 and 7. In the Core paper there are 10 marks for each exercise, making a total of 20, while in the Extended paper there are 18 marks for each exercise, making a total of 36. Exercises 6 and 7 therefore represent a large part of the total number of marks available in the exam: 20 out of 56 for the Core paper, and 36 out of 84 for the Extended. It is important that you give yourself enough time to answer the two questions well, without having to rush or perhaps even having to leave one question unfinished. The marks are divided equally between marks for language and marks for content.

What are the assessment objectives?

In Exercises 6 and 7 only writing skills are assessed and therefore there are **no** Reading assessment objectives. For both the Core and Extended papers, you are assessed on your ability to:

- communicate clearly, accurately and appropriately (Writing assessment objective 1)
- convey information and express opinions effectively (W2)
- employ and control a variety of grammatical structures (W3)
- demonstrate knowledge and understanding of a range of appropriate vocabulary (W4)
- observe conventions of paragraphing, punctuation and spelling (W5)
- employ appropriate register/style (W6).

Check!

Look back at the Check exercise on page **83** in the Exercise 5 unit to check you understand what the Writing assessment objectives mean. The answers are provided in the key.

What do Exercises 6 and 7 look like?

In both the Core and Extended papers, the text of the questions will look like the ones on page **107**, but will include some pictures and bullet points for Exercise 6 and some speech bubbles for Exercise 7. This is followed by a full page of lines for you to write your answer on. Remember that the purpose, format and audience for the two questions will be different; in other words, if you have to write something informal for Exercise 6, then Exercise 7 will require a more formal type of writing. Also, if you write a letter in Exercise 6, then Exercise 7 will normally ask you to produce a different type of writing, such as a report, a speech or an article, and **not** another letter.

What's the difference between the Core and Extended papers?

The only difference between the Core and Extended papers is the number of words which you need to write. For the Core paper you should write between 100 and 150 words for each exercise; for the Extended paper, between 150 and 200 words. However, the questions are the same for both papers.

What do I need to know?

Your writing is marked for both its **content** (your ideas and how you develop them, and if you have thought about the purpose, audience and register) and for its **language** (the style and accuracy of what you write, and how simple or complex the vocabulary and sentence structures are).

Check!

Do you think the following comments apply to content (C) or language (L)?

- material is correct length _____
- simple structures and vocabulary _____
- grammatical mistakes _____
- no paragraphs, or paragraphs not consistent _____
- some repetition of ideas _____
- no understanding of the task _____
- incorrect register _____
- meaning is clear _____
- does not quite answer the question _____
- includes topics which are not relevant _____

If your writing is a lot shorter than the necessary word limit, it will probably not get more than two or three marks for content because it will not have answered the question. There will not be enough detail or development.

Exercise 6

There are usually some pictures on the question page of Exercise 6. These are there as prompts to give you ideas to write about, but you may prefer to use an idea of your own instead. If you use the pictures, you should choose one idea from one picture and develop it (**don't** write a brief description of each picture).

You must try to write something for **all three** bullet points in the question. If you do not try to answer all three points you will not be given high marks for content, because you will not have answered the full question.

Exercise 7

In Exercise 7, there are four prompts in speech bubbles, usually in the form of comments from friends or colleagues. Two of the prompts are for (agree with) the proposal in the title and two are against (disagree with) the proposal. You can choose to use these ideas or ideas of your own. If you do use the ideas in the prompts, try to use your own words rather than copying them directly. It is better to use only one or two of the prompts and develop them rather than write brief details about each one.

Remember!

- Think about the purpose, format and audience before you write.
- You will write one formal and one informal piece of writing in the two exercises. You should use the correct register (formal or informal style).
- In the Core paper write between 100 and 150 words.
- In the Extended paper write between 150 and 200 words.
- It is your writing skills that are being assessed, **not** your reading skills.
- Your writing is marked for both content and language.
- In Exercise 6 you must answer **all** of the bullet points.

B Preparation

Activity 1

Look at this Exercise 6, which asks you to write an informal letter. Then answer the questions below.

EXTENDED

Exercise 6

You have just completed some volunteer work during your school holidays.

Write a letter to a good friend about the experience.

In your letter you should:

- mention what the work was and why you did it
- describe the main duty that you had to perform and with whom
- say how you felt about the whole experience.

Your letter should be between 150 and 200 words long. Do not write an address.

You will receive up to 9 marks for the content of your letter, and up to 9 marks for the style and accuracy of your language.

---

a   What format is needed for your answer?

b   What are you going to write about?

c   Who are you going to write to?

d   Will the style be formal or informal?

e   What will make the audience think that it is a good piece of writing?

_____
_____
_____
_____
_____
_____

Activity 2

Before you can begin writing, you need to think very carefully about **what** you are going to write. It is a good idea to make notes first so that it will be much easier to start writing.

Think about

- the name of the good friend you are writing to
- **what** the volunteer work was
- **why** you did the volunteer work
- the main duties of the work
- **how you felt** about the work.

Activity 3

Think about the start of your letter. What is the best way to begin?

_____

Activity 4

How many main sections or paragraphs do you think your letter should have? Why? What information will go in each paragraph?

_____
_____
_____

Activity 5

Here is a possible plan for your answer to the question in Activity **1**:

Paragraph	Content
1	General introduction, state reason for writing to friend (**purpose**)
2	Mention the volunteer work and say why you did it
3	Describe the main duties that you had to perform and with whom
4	Say how you felt about the whole experience
5	Closing

Note that you may find the second, third and fourth paragraphs could be just two paragraphs, depending on how you write your answer.

Decide which of the following makes the better opening for your letter. Why?

1

Dear Sam

I've just completed some volunteer work during the school holidays and I'm writing to tell you about it. I worked in a youth centre downtown for a month because I wanted to find out what it is like working with children. I was in charge of sports activities.

2

Dear Sam

How are you? I hope everything is OK with you and your family. How's your little sister? Is she better now? Sorry I haven't been in touch recently but that's why I'm writing to you now, to tell you about some volunteer work I took on during the school holidays.

Activity 6

Complete this sample second paragraph of the letter by putting each of the verbs in brackets into the correct tense for events that have happened.

I **(a)** _____ (always want) to work with children but so far I **(b)** _____ (not have) any real opportunities to do this. Both my mum and dad **(c)** _____ (be) teachers and before the last summer holidays they **(d)** _____ (tell) me that a local youth organisation **(e)** _____ (need) volunteer workers during the holidays. I **(f)** _____ (decide) that this would be an excellent opportunity for me to get some experience working with children, and so I **(g)** _____ (apply) and luckily for me they **(h)** _____ (accept) my application!

Notice that we often only need two tenses to give news: the **present perfect** simple and the **past** simple.

Activity 7

Use the words below to write the third paragraph of the letter, adding words if needed. Put the verbs into the correct tense. From the plan in Activity **5**, the ideas for the third and fourth paragraphs have been combined into one paragraph.

> I / be / really / thrilled / and / although / work / not / very / difficult / I / have / lot / fun
>
> _____
>
> _____
>
> At / start / I / have / arrange / programme / sports / activities / children/ and / decide / equipment / be / needed / each activity
>
> _____
>
> _____
>
> The organisers / give / me / small amount / money / it / be / my / responsibility / go / shops / buy / all / different equipment
>
> _____
>
> _____
>
> And then for / rest / time / I / help / children / with / various sports. They / play / football, basketball, and volleyball and some / them / go / swim
>
> _____
>
> _____

Activity 8

Now write the final paragraph.

_____

_____

_____

_____

_____

_____

_____

_____

Activity 9

Look at this Exercise 7 (Core) question. Then answer the questions below.

Exercise 7

Your school principal is proposing that each pupil reduces wastage at your school.

Here are some comments from students in your school:

'I think the school staff members are the most wasteful – think about all those exam papers!'

'If we start reducing wastage at school, maybe we can do the same at home and even save some money.'

'I'm so bored of all this talk about waste at school! Just look at all the wastage in supermarkets and shops!'

'What a great idea! Finally we teenagers can teach the adults something about helping the environment!'

As a member of the student council you have been asked to write an article for your school magazine about the issue.

Your article should be between 100 and 150 words long.

The comments above may give you some ideas but you are free to use any ideas of your own.

You will receive up to 5 marks for the content of your article, and up to 5 marks for the style and accuracy of your language.

a   What format is needed for your answer?

b   What are you going to write about?

c   Who are you going to write to?

d   Will the style be formal or informal?

e   What will make the audience think that it is a good piece of writing?

_____

_____

_____

_____

_____

Activity 10

Before you can begin writing, you need to think very carefully about **what** you are going to write. It is a good idea to make notes first so that it will be much easier to start writing.

Think about the following questions.

- How do you feel about doing more to reduce wastage in your school? What are the advantages and disadvantages?
- Do you agree or disagree with the comments from students in your school? Why?
- How could you reduce wastage in your school? Make a list of the things you could do.

Activity 11

Make a plan for your writing. Use the plan in Activity **5** to help you.

Paragraph	Content
1	
2	
3	
4	

Activity 12

How similar is your plan to this one?

Paragraph	Content
1	General introduction to the topic, both sides of the argument
2	Agreeing with the proposal: one advantage
3	Disagreeing with proposal: one disadvantage
4	Conclusion, balancing the discussion, giving your own opinion about the proposal

It is recommended that you choose **one** advantage and **one** disadvantage only. You should then develop them rather than trying to cover all four prompts briefly. You should expand on the points you choose and include your own ideas about the proposal.

Remember!

- Make notes before you begin writing.
- Plan your answer.
- In Exercise 6, answer **all** of the bullet points.
- In Exercise 7 you can use the prompts in the speech bubbles or your own ideas.
- If you use the speech bubble prompts, try to change the words.
- Use a topic sentence to introduce each paragraph.

Activity 13

Paragraphs often begin with an introductory sentence, called a **topic sentence**, which lets the reader know what the paragraph is going to be about. Match these topic sentences with the four paragraphs in Activity **12**.

a However, there may be problems for some young people if they are asked to do something like this. _____

b Overall, this is an excellent proposal which I think everyone in our school should support. _____

c Nowadays, wastage is causing environmental problems all over the world. _____

d Spending time thinking about the problem of wastage has several advantages. _____

Activity 14

Using your notes from Activity **10**, and what you have learnt from Activities **11–13**, expand on the topic sentences to make four short paragraphs of about 30–40 words each.

1 _____
_____
_____
_____

2 _____
_____
_____
_____

3 _____
_____
_____
_____

4 _____
_____
_____
_____

C Exam focus

Informal writing

You are going to look at some sample answers from IGCSE students to the following IGCSE examination question:

Exercise 6

You recently moved to a different town and have just finished your first week at a new school.

Write a letter to a friend about your new situation.

Don't forget to include:

- how you feel about your new town
- how your new school differs from the old school
- details about a person that you have made friends with.

Your letter should be between 100 and 150 (Core) / 150 and 200 (Extended) words long. Do not write an address.

You will receive up to 5 (Core) / 9 (Extended) marks for the content of your letter, and up to 5 (Core) / 9 (Extended) marks for the style and accuracy of your language.

Source: Cambridge IGCSE E2L (0510/21) Oct/Nov 2008, page 12, Exercise 6

Activity 15

Before you read the sample answers, read the question carefully. What are the **purpose**, **format** and **audience**?

_____

_____

_____

Activity 16

Look at the three sample answers that follow (**1–3**). Decide which are the best and worst answers, and say why. Think about both content and language.

1

Dear

I hope you're fine. I have just moved to a different town and I'm writing to tell you about the whole situation.

The new town is quite good and offers you many things to do, but I miss the old town very much. The neighborhood I live now has everywhere parks and playgrounds, like the old one, but the only difference is that there are plants in every home. You think that you live in countryside.

My new school is in much better condition that the school I used to go, with excellent facilities that make the lessons more pleasant. The chemistry laboratory is one of my favorite places that I spent most of my time in school.

Also, I started to make new friends. Few days ago I met Mary, is my partner in chemistry. She showed me all the places that I can go when I have free time. She's very pleasant as person and she has a great sense of humour.

I hope that one day you can visit me and I'll show you my new favourite places and also I'll meet you Mary. I'm sure that we will have a great time.

Kisses,

2

Dear

Hello! How are you? Is your family alright? I miss you all so much. So I'm writing to you in order to tell you my news.

Moving to a different town and even going to a new school made me a little upset as I'm a long way away from friends. However, I have to say that this town is beautiful. It might not have so many clubs and cafe' as my old town but it has a lovely park, full of green and a shopping centre with cinema.

Furthermore, the school is pretty nice here. It's small but it's full of nice people. Students and professors. Of course my previous school is bigger with more facilities and with all my friends going there.

It's a little bit hard for me making new friends now, however, I got really closed with the girl sitting next to me. Her name is Aristi. She came from another town, too. She's really nice and helps me with everything.

That's all. Please write back soon telling me your news. Don't forget to give my regards to your family.

With love,

3 Dear

I have just finished my first week at a new school and I am writing you to express my feelings. Even though I haven't got completely used to my new town, I am pleased with it because it has beautiful, opened, large green areas, lots of near-by services and an overall young population. I am therefore grateful to my parents because I known they are doing all of this to improve my life.

My first day at school was a complete success as everyone received me with a warm smile. However, it is more strict and teachers always keep an eye on whatever it is you are doing. I guess it will take some time for me to change, but I actually like it because they are turning me into a more serious person, highly prepared for the future.

Talking about friends, I am feeling very comfortable around these new people. These are almost no prejudices and everybody is willing to have a pleasant conversation with you anytime. I have actually become a very close friend to a sixteen year-old girl whose name is Mary. Even though she will never replace you, we have lots of fun together, and she is someone who always listens to me! So, I am actually feeling like in home. How are things around there? Best wishes,

---

Activity 17

Look at the examiners' comments for the three sample answers in Activity **16**. Match the answers (**1–3**) with the comments below (**a–c**). Give reasons for your choices.

a Content

The writing answers all three bullet points and answers the question with relevant and informal language. It is clear that the writer is thinking about the person who will read the letter, especially with the personalised introduction and final paragraph. The ideas are quite simple but the candidate has tried to develop them. The whole piece is interesting to read although it sometimes repeats information.

Language

The candidate sometimes tries to use more unusual and complex phrases and expressions. The use of vocabulary is mainly correct, although there are some basic small mistakes. There is a good balance to the whole piece with three paragraphs, each describing one of the bullet points, and two short but informal opening and concluding paragraphs.

b Content

This writing fully answers the question. All three bullet points are answered and developed well. The candidate has expressed his/her own ideas which are original and complex. The whole piece is very enjoyable and interesting to read.

Language

The style is confident and the candidate is comfortable with using complex expressions. There is good use of idioms and tenses. There are very few mistakes and the whole piece is highly accurate. The candidate uses connecting words and phrases very well. The paragraphs are well constructed and focus clearly on each of the three bullet points.

c Content

The writing covers all three bullet points using a good language style. The start and conclusion include a personal element. The ideas are developed and the candidate offers some additional detail to support them. The details are quite basic but the whole piece includes some interesting information.

Language

The candidate uses simple structures and vocabulary, and sometimes tries to use more complex expressions. The meaning is clear and spelling is generally correct. There are some mistakes including verb tenses, missing words such as articles (e.g. the, an), and incorrect choice of vocabulary. The letter is well balanced and the five paragraphs are used well.

More formal writing

You are going to look at some sample answers from IGCSE students to the following IGCSE examination question:

Exercise 7

A local newspaper is inviting young people to write an article about the use of mobile phones and their advantages and disadvantages.

Here are some comments your friends made when you were researching the topic:

'I feel safer having my phone with me when I'm out.'

'Mobile phones are noisy and annoying in public places.'

'I can get in touch with my friends at any time.'

'We still aren't sure about the health risks connected with these phones.'

> **Write an article for your local newspaper giving your views about the issue.**
>
> **Your article should be between 100 and 150 (Core) / 150 and 200 (Extended) words long.**
>
> The comments above may give you some ideas but you are free to use any ideas of your own.
>
> You will receive up to 5 (Core) / 9 (Extended) marks for the content of your article, and up to 5 (Core) / 9 (Extended) marks for the style and accuracy of your language.

Source: Cambridge IGCSE E2L (0510/12) Oct/Nov 2008, page 12, Exercise 7

Activity 18

Before you read the sample answers, read the question carefully. What are the **purpose**, **format** and **audience**?

_____

_____

_____

Activity 19

Look at the three sample answers that follow (**1–3**). Decide which are the best and worst answers, and say why. Think about both content and language.

1

We live in the age of huge progress in the domain of communication. One of the biggest inventions is the mobile phone. But how useful or harmful is for us and certainly for our health.

From the one hand, mobile phones are very practical and make our lives easier. We can communicate with our friends or our relatives even when we are miles away without using telephones with wires. Furthermore, we can sent messages, images and ringtones to another device and using this way of communication we can 'speak' with our friends without talking. Another thing we should mention is that this device is small and easy to carry it with you.

But from the other hand, there are also problems caused by cell phones. Mainly health problems. Many people, mostly students claim that they suffer from terrible headaches and some of them often feel dizzy. Also, mobile phones can be harmful for those people who have problems with their heart or their heart is being supported by a device. Many people feel pain in their fingers because of using their cell phones often.

To sum up we know that cell phones are very useful but also they could risk our health, so we should use it but with a limit.

(2) Mobile phones seem to be everywhere. Nowadays almost everybody over the age of 11 owns one, and many people wonder whether it is a positive or negative influence.

I think that most of the people agree that these objects have advantages and disadvantages. On one hand, they are considered to be very useful because of the fast communication you can have at any moment. Many of us affirm that it is safer to move with mobile phones because, in case of emergencies, you can quickly call somebody to help you. it is also said that they are practical because you can get in touch with your friends, send text messages, and with today's technology, listen to some music, take pictures, and many more.

However, there are some negative aspects that disturb people. We can say that mobile phones become annoying when they ring in public places because they usually interrupt moments. Moreover, many people disagree with their use because they consider that it can affect health, increasing the risks in human beings. Finally, we can say that many people do not give the phone its appropriate use and therefore, it can badly influence behaviours.

So, are people willing to forget the disadvantages and continue using them, or are we willing to sacrifice communication in order to keep a spontaneous life?

(3) The mobile phones are a relatively new invention which was introduced as recently are early eighties. However, a personal mobile phones become a common item nowadays. We can't imagine a life without this invention and possibly bring a tremendous chaos to the world.

A mobile technology is developed further and now this contributes many advantages. Some people feel safer when they have phones and outside of home. Regardless of distance, a person can get in touch with his friends at any time. Many business officers are strengthened as they can gain is information by communicating on phone-pertinent to the importance of mobile phones.

Some, doubt the phones are good. The reasons because mobile phones are noisy and annoying in public places. Often, people believes about the health risks connected with those items.

In conclusion, I wish to say it is of great advantage having this technology because without this is, just like a bicycle without another pedal. It works but not well in out lifetime.

Activity 20

Look at the examiners' comments for the three sample answers in Activity **19**. Match the answers (**1–3**) with the comments that follow (**a–c**). Give reasons for your choices.

a Content

The candidate has tried to answer the question and use of language is accurate and formal. Several ideas are expressed in connection with the advantages and disadvantages, but they are not well developed and the ideas are not well ordered. This means that the argument does not always seem to be complete. The final paragraph tries to conclude the candidate's argument but is confusing.

Language

The candidate tries to use a variety of language and expression and spelling is fine. Unfortunately, there are many basic mistakes which make the piece difficult to understand and slow down reading. Many of these mistakes are serious and involve subject/verb agreement (e.g. people believes*), the wrong use of articles (such as* a, the, *and so on) and some phrases which are difficult to understand. However, they do not stop communication and paragraphs are used well.*

b Content

The candidate answers the question and focuses clearly on the advantages and disadvantages. The writing style is formal and it is clear who the writer is writing to. The candidate has used the ideas in the speech bubble prompts but has developed them well, and has included some of his/her own ideas. The quality of the piece is continued throughout and the open question at the end is a nice touch, making the reader continue to think.

Language

The sentences are varied in length and the candidate has used complex language in places. The vocabulary is generally accurate and shows variety. The whole piece is generally grammatically accurate. The four paragraphs provide a good balance to the article, with an introduction, conclusion and a section on both the advantages and disadvantages.

c Content

The piece answers the question and the candidate has tried to cover both the advantages and disadvantages. The language used in the article is generally formal. However, when the candidate writes about the health problems, the language becomes rather informal. The candidate has used the ideas in the speech bubble prompts but has tried to reword and develop them. The short final paragraph provides a balanced conclusion to the whole piece.

Language

The grammatical structures and the choice of vocabulary are safe and satisfactory, and the candidate has tried to use some more complex language. The meaning is clear and the message is communicated. There are a few spelling mistakes and some expressions which show that the candidate is not always confident in the use of language. The four paragraphs provide a good balance to the whole article.

Exam practice

1 CORE AND EXTENDED

> ## Exercise 6
>
> **You recently saw a film on TV or at the cinema.**
>
> **Write a letter to a friend about the film.**
>
> Don't forget to include:
> - the name of the film and the main actors, and where you saw it
> - what the film was about
> - say if you would recommend the film to your friend.
>
> **Your letter should be between 100 and 150 (Core) / 150 and 200 (Extended) words long. Do not write an address.**
>
> You will receive up to 5 (Core) / 9 (Extended) marks for the content of your letter, and up to 5 (Core) / 9 (Extended) marks for the style and accuracy of your language.

[Total: 10 or 18]

> ### Exercise 6
>
> **You have just taken part in a community festival to celebrate an important date in your country's history.**
>
> **Write a letter to a friend telling him or her about the festival.**
>
> In your letter include:
> - what the festival was about, and when it happened
> - what you did during the festival
> - your feelings about the festival.
>
> **Your letter should be between 100 and 150 (Core) / 150 and 200 (Extended) words long. Do not write an address.**
>
> You will receive up to 5 (Core) / 9 (Extended) marks for the content of your letter, and up to 5 (Core) / 9 (Extended) marks for the style and accuracy of your language.

[Total: 10 or 18]

Exercise 6

Your school has been invited to send a team of students to take part in an international sports event.

Write an article for your school newsletter, telling the students about the event.

In your article you need to tell them:

- when and where the sports event is taking place
- what sports are included
- how they can apply and how members will be chosen.

Your article should be between 100 and 150 (Core) / 150 and 200 (Extended) words long. Do not write an address.

You will receive up to 5 (Core) / 9 (Extended) marks for the content of your article, and up to 5 (Core) / 9 (Extended) marks for the style and accuracy of your language.

[Total: 10 or 18]

Exercise 6

A family member you haven't seen for some years is planning to visit you and your family.

Write a letter to this family member telling him or her:
- how much you are looking forward to his/her visit
- what new things you have become interested in
- what you would like to do together when you meet.

Your letter should be between 100 and 150 (Core) / 150 and 200 (Extended) words long. Do not write an address.

You will receive up to 5 (Core) / 9 (Extended) marks for the content of your letter, and up to 5 (Core) / 9 (Extended) marks for the style and accuracy of your language.

[Total: 10 or 18]

Exercise 7

These days, more and more people are using bicycles as an alternative method of transport.

Here are some comments your friends made when you were researching the topic:

'I feel much healthier if I use my bicycle instead of my parents' car.'

'There is so much traffic on the roads that I'm really frightened of riding my bicycle to school.'

'It might take a little longer, but the benefits to the environment make it worthwhile.'

'It's OK to ride when the sun is shining, but what about when the weather is bad?'

Write an article for your local newspaper giving your views about the issue.

Your article should be between 100 and 150 (Core) / 150 and 200 (Extended) words long.

The comments above may give you some ideas but you are free to use any ideas of your own.

You will receive up to 5 (Core) / 9 (Extended) marks for the content of your article, and up to 5 (Core) / 9 (Extended) marks for the style and accuracy of your language.

[Total: 10 or 18]

Exercise 7

Your local newspaper is asking for views on ways to help people in need in other countries.

Here are some comments received about the subject:

'I think we should help people here at home first – there are many people who need help in my country.'

'We have so much and some people have so little – does it really hurt us to help others?'

'If I send money or clothes for people in need in other countries, it worries me that my help might go to the wrong people.'

'My plan is to work overseas in the future and help people in need. I don't care what I do, but I know that I want to help.'

Write an article for your local newspaper giving your views about the issue.

Your article should be between 100 and 150 (Core) / 150 and 200 (Extended) words long.

The comments above may give you some ideas but you are free to use any ideas of your own.

You will receive up to 5 (Core) / 9 (Extended) marks for the content of your article, and up to 5 (Core) / 9 (Extended) marks for the style and accuracy of your language.

[Total: 10 or 18]

Exercise 7

Your school/college is preparing a project about smoking.

Here are some comments your friends made when you were researching the topic:

'If someone wants to smoke and get ill, that's his or her choice.'

'I think there should be special places where people can smoke if they want to.'

'Smoking is a terrible habit which causes many social problems and can even kill you — it should be banned!'

'Why doesn't the government increase taxes on smoking and use this money to pay for medical care when smokers need it?'

Your teacher has asked you to write an article for the project giving your views about the issue.

Your article should be between 100 and 150 (Core) / 150 and 200 (Extended) words long.

The comments above may give you some ideas but you are free to use any ideas of your own.

You will receive up to 5 (Core) / 9 (Extended) marks for the content of your article, and up to 5 (Core) / 9 (Extended) marks for the style and accuracy of your language.

[Total: 10 or 18]

Exercise 7

Advertising is an important part of life in the 21st century, but is this good or bad?

Write a letter to your local newspaper giving your views about the topic.

'Adverts help us to choose what to buy, so what's wrong with that?'

'I think advertisements in the media help to make the news more interesting!'

'Nobody really believes what adverts tell us.'

'The problem with adverts is that they encourage us to buy things that we don't really want, and which we probably can't afford.'

Your letter should be between 100 and 150 (Core) / 150 and 200 (Extended) words long.

The comments above may give you some ideas but you are free to use any ideas of your own.

You will receive up to 5 (Core) / 9 (Extended) marks for the content of your letter, and up to 5 (Core) / 9 (Extended) marks for the style and accuracy of your language.

[Total: 10 or 18]

Exercises 1 and 2: Key

A Introduction

Check!

Skimming is to get a general picture of a text. *Scanning* is to get a deeper understanding of a text.

Check!

Infer means to form an opinion about something based on information that you have read or listened to.

B Preparation

Activity 1

a   We know the text is about whale safaris (from the heading and the question).

b   The layout helps you find information because of the paragraphs and the headings.

c   Possible answers (two needed for each section): *Where?* – location, specific places; *The experience* – excitement, emotions, things to see; *The environment* – climate, sea, mountains; *Safari options* – types of safari, group safaris.

Activity 4

(b) and **(f)**   2 details needed for 1 mark

(e)   2 details needed, 2 marks available

Be careful to give two details, not just one, if the question asks for two.

Activities 5 and 6

Students' own answers

Activity 7

Question	Section	Reason
(a)	Where?	because the question asks 'when' (at what time of year) – probably in same place in text as it gives information about 'where'
(b)	The experience	because question asks about 'other types of wildlife' – seeing other wildlife is probably part of the experience
(c)	The experience	probably getting information is part of the experience
(d)	The environment	question mentions the Arctic

Activity 8

There are three paragraphs.

Activity 9

(e)–(g) All the answers are probably in the *Safari options* section.

Activity 10

(a) 5   **(b)** 4   **(c)** 7   **(d)** 3   **(e) (i)** and **(ii)** 2   **(f)** 6   **(g)** 1

Activity 11

a   We know the text is about travelling from London to Paris (from the heading and the question).

b   The layout helps you find information because of the paragraphs and the headings.

c   Possible answers (two needed for each section): *Train from London to Europe by Eurostar* – speed, travel time; *Somewhere magical* – places to visit, things to do; *Easy to book, easy to travel* – ways to book, prices, times.

Activity 14

(b) and **(f)**   2 details needed for 1 mark

Activities 15 and 16

Students' own answers

Activity 17

Question	Section	Reason
(a)	Train from London to Europe by Eurostar	because the question does not really match the other two paragraphs; also, first question, first paragraph
(b)	Train from London to Europe by Eurostar	asks what can you do on the train, so answer likely to be in this paragraph
(c)	Train from London to Europe by Eurostar OR Easy to book, easy to travel	both possible as question asks for travel information (answer is actually in 'somewhere magical')
(d)	Somewhere magical	question mentions Disneyland
(e)	Easy to book, easy to travel	this paragraph very likely as the question mentions getting help
(f)	Easy to book, easy to travel	the question asks for ways to book a ticket

Activity 18

(a) 5   **(b)** 3   **(c)** 2   **(d)** 6   **(e)** 4   **(f)** 1

Activity 19

a   Smaller font, more text, no paragraph headings

b   Diagram

Activity 21

(a)	2 details needed for 1 mark
(c), (d) and **(f)**	2 details needed for 2 marks
(h)	4 details needed, 4 marks available

Activities 22 and 23

Students' own answers

Activity 24

Answer **1** as it is short and clear.

Activity 25

Lanterns are lights. It is not necessary to fully understand the word *lanterns* to answer the question.

Activity 26

An *obstacle* is something which blocks your path or stops you from doing what you want to do.

Activity 27

The answer should include **(i)** gave guidance/help in the cave, **(ii)** provided caving equipment.

Activity 28

1.25 km

Activity 29

(i) black soot from lamps

(ii) removed stones from the walls

Activity 30

that beauty will be preserved **or** people's bad habits will disappear

Activity 31

commercial buildings / food stalls / concrete walkways / rubbish left behind / quiet atmosphere disappeared (**four** details needed)

C Exam focus

Activity 32

Students' own answers

Activity 33

CORE

(a) 3 details needed for 1 mark

(e) 2 details required for 1 mark

EXTENDED

(a) 3 details needed for 1 mark

(b) 2 details required for 2 marks

(f) 2 details required for 1 mark

(b) in the Extended paper does not appear in the Core paper

Activity 34

Students' own answers

Activity 35

CORE

(a) rice, wheat and maize

(b) oil

(c) flavour

(d) provide shade

(e) keeps freshness of fruits / eco-friendly / stops fruits from getting squashed (2 details for 1 mark)

(f) bring luck / prosperity

EXTENDED

(a) rice, wheat and maize

(b) **(i)** hygienic, **(ii)** environmentally friendly / environmental

(c) oil

(d) flavour

(e) provide shade

(f) keeps freshness of fruits / eco-friendly / stops fruits from getting squashed (2 details for 1 mark)

(g) bring luck / prosperity

Activity 36

The best answer is **3**, followed by answer **4**, then **2** and the worst is **1**.

Activity 37

1 b   **2** d   **3** c   **4** a

Activity 38

1 3   **2** 5   **3** 8   **4** 6

Activity 39

The graph gives information about life expectancy in Europe for males and females, with dates and age in years. There is an obvious link with the text title *Soon we may live for 200 years*.

Activity 40

Questions **(b)** and **(d)** (2 marks each) and **(j)** (4 marks) require more than one piece of information.

Question **(f)** asks you to look at the graph.

Activity 41

Students' own answers

Activity 42

(a) has almost doubled

(b) **(i)** growing new teeth from stem cells, **(ii)** developing drugs to imitate effects of eating less

(c) longest recorded life span / lived to be 122 years old / lived 1875–1997

(d) **(i)** cleaner living conditions, **(ii)** discovery of life-saving medicines

(e) stop repairing themselves

(f) five years

(g) because of cancer, heart disease, major health problems / complete removal of major diseases is slow

(h) do something more with our lives / achieve more of our dreams / achieve more of our potential

(j) Predictions: **two** of **(i)** average life expectancy to 200 years / living to 200 years, **(ii)** start middle age on 100th birthday, **(iii)** double life span

Effects: **two** of **(iv)** reduce calorie intake, **(v)** people stay healthier, **(vi)** fewer overweight people

Activity 43

The best answer is **3**, followed by answer **4**, then **1**, and the worst is **2**.

Activity 44

1 b   2 d   3 c   4 a

Activity 45

1 6   2 5   3 13   4 11

D Exam practice

EXERCISE 1

1 CORE

(a) children to seniors

(b) explore coastline by climbing, jumping from sea cliffs and swimming in the waves

(c) 7

(d) with basic skills

(e) €20

(f) three of: towel, packed lunch, drink, sun block

2 EXTENDED

(a) 65 acres

(b) every half hour

(c) during the winter months

(d) park admission and party bags

(e) 'Vegetarian Jungle Picnic'

(f) two of: photo of your chosen animal / an adoption certificate / a year's free entry to Monkey World

(g) Adoption Centre

3 CORE AND EXTENDED

(a) two of: runny or blocked nose / sneezing / watery eyes

(b) two of: flowers / tree blossom / grass

(c) eczema, asthma

(d) two of: sleeping / making decisions / playing outside / school performance (exams)

(e) symptoms often lessen or completely disappear during adulthood

(f) two of: check the pollen forecast / stay indoors with the windows shut on days when the pollen count is high / spend little time outdoors during peak pollen times / if you have been outside, change your clothes and have a shower / start medicines ahead of pollen season

EXERCISE 2

4 CORE AND EXTENDED

(a) legs and backbone

(b) they are more likely to suffer from arthritis

(c) South and Central America

(d) west

(e) animals that eat the toads die from their poison, toads take over natural habitats of native species

(f) Northern Territory

(g) they do not travel as fast or as far, they are less likely to suffer from arthritis

(h) in the laboratory they would travel less distance with each hop, arthritis didn't slow down toads outside the laboratory

(i) 1935 – yellow toads introduced in Queensland, attempt to stop insects destroying crops; 1990s – poison virus tried to remove toads, also killed native frogs

5 CORE AND EXTENDED

(a) it may contain precious metals

(b) used in new electronic parts; sold to jewellers, investors and manufacturers; used in circuit boards

(c) gold conducts electricity better than copper

(d) about 5 grams per tonne of ore from the ground, compared to 150 grams per tonne of discarded mobile phones

(e) reduces the need to import more precious metals

(f) increased

(g) to some people old phones and electronics are just a mountain of rubbish, but to Yamanaka's company they are a mountain of gold

(h) because of competition from China

(i) flat panel televisions and computer screens

(j) two of: they put them away and forget about them / worried about personal data stored on phones / phones are personal items / top of range phones expensive to buy / feel better if they keep phones as long as possible

6 CORE AND EXTENDED

(a) for local fishermen and other sailors

(b) 4

(c) small part from rear end

(d) to complete his boat before the next summer tourist season starts, because losing the boat hurts terribly

(e) none **or** just him

(f) friends, family, municipality

(g) 30

(h) there are no young boat builders / there are only older boat builders 70+ years

(i) many boats are imported from abroad, there are no special factories or boat yards in Cyprus

(j) given small piece of land, electricity, water, small hut

Exercise 3: Key

A Introduction

Check!

1 information presented in a variety of forms	e You will read texts taken from advertisements, articles, magazines, reports, etc.
2 select and organise material	d You need to choose the right information from the texts and arrange it correctly.
3 communicate clearly, accurately and appropriately	c The things you write should be easy to read and understand.
4 infer information	b Sometimes when you read you may need to guess what something means.
5 observe conventions	a Your writing should follow the rules.

Check!

The main difference is that the Core text is <u>slightly shorter</u> than the Extended text. In the <u>Core</u> paper you need to write **two** sentences in the <u>final section</u>.

Check!

deleting	~~breakfast~~
underlining	<u>football</u>
circling	(14–16 years)
ticking	male ✓
capital letters	LONDON

B **Preparation**

Activity 3

e person's name

b name of the building, like an apartment building, and room number (if necessary)

d house number, street

a town/village, city, prefecture/state/province

c postal code / zip code, country

Activity 4

Giovanni Politti is an Italian citizen who was born in Milan but now lives in **(a)** Rome. He lives in **(d)** via Colosseo at **(b)** building 56A, in apartment 311. The postal code for his address is **(c)** 00876.

Activity 5

Family name: Politti

First name: Giovanni

Full address: Apartment 311, Building 56A, via Colosseo, 00876 Rome (Italy)

Activities 6 and 7

First name: Nina

Family name: Sciapoulos

Full address: 47 Koronis, Chalandrion, Athens, Greece

Email: sciapo2@systema.gr

Telephone: 143769045

Activity 8

The text provides information about:

accommodation

meals

food allergies

methods of travel

holiday dates

length of holiday

excursions and sightseeing.

Accommodation: (please tick your preference)

☑ Hotel ☐ Apartment ☐ Camping

Travel: (please tick your preference)

☐ Car ☐ Aeroplane ☑ Train

Preferred departure day: (please circle)

Sunday (Wednesday) Saturday

Preferred departure time: (please circle)

Morning (Afternoon) Evening

Other requirements: (please delete) **Note**: these must be booked in advance

Car hire ~~Yes~~/No   Guide services Yes/~~No~~

Activity 11

a   Written in wrong person

b   Too long

c   Two sentences

d   Too short

e   Two sentences and some wrong information

C   Exam focus

Activity 12

Paragraph 1 – family name, age, address, previous volunteer work, countries

Paragraph 2 – previous camp experience

Paragraph 3 – days at camp, lessons taught, other activities, skills

Paragraph 4 – what he was impressed by

Paragraph 5 – disadvantages

Paragraph 6 – future teaching career

Paragraph 7 – giving feedback

Activity 13

Surname and Initial – 1

Address and Age – 1

Time spent at camp – 3

Activities taught – 3

Age group taught – 1

Number of children in group – 4

Most students came from – 1

Did you experience any problems …? – 5

Would you like to work at the camp in the future? – 6

What would your preferences be …? – 5

Activity 14

Answer **1** is the best, followed by **2**, and the least successful is **3**.

Activity 15

1 b   **2 c**   **3 a**

D   Exam practice

1 CORE

Sports club membership form

SECTION A – Personal details

Full name: <u>Maria Alexandrou</u>   [1]

Address: <u>9 Edesis Street, Kaimakli, Nicosia 1022 (Cyprus)</u>   [1]

Email: <u>mariaa@cymail.eu</u>   Mobile: <u>99386772</u>   [1]

Age next birthday: <u>17</u>   [1]

SECTION B – Sports

Please tick your preferred sport (only **one**):   [1]

☐ gymnastics ☐ tennis ☑ football ☐ swimming ☐ basketball ☐ volleyball

Give details of experience in your preferred sport:

<u>Junior girls' team for 3 years</u>   [1]

Please tick any other sports which you enjoy: [1]

☐ gymnastics ☐ tennis ☐ football ✓ swimming ✓ basketball ✓ volleyball

SECTION C – Days, times & fees

On which days do you want to visit the club? Please circle all that apply. [1]

Mon (Tue) (Wed) Thu Fri (Sat) Sun

At what time do you want to visit the club? Please circle all that apply. [1]

(Morning) Afternoon (Evening)

Please tick the weekly fee which applies to you. [1]

✓ 10 euros ☐ 15 euros ☐ 20 euros

Are you applying for a student discount? Please delete. [1]

YES / ~~NO~~

What proof of identity are you providing? Please circle. [1]

(Letter) Student Card

SECTION D

In the space below, write **one** sentence about how you will travel to the club and **one** sentence about your plans for the future.

(Possible answer) I will cycle to the club on my bike. My plan is to play football in a senior team so that I can travel abroad to different countries. [4]

2 EXTENDED

Holiday feedback form

SECTION A – Personal details

Family name Jawali [1]

Adults' (18+) first names: Kamal, Ahmed, Jamila [1]

Home address: Apartment 698, Block F3, Al Fazari Street, Riyadh (Saudi Arabia) [1]

Email: jawali@saudi.email.net   Home phone: 38219587 [1]

SECTION B – Holiday details

Name of hotel and destination: Regent Hotel, Cairo [1]

Travel dates from 25 July to 3 August

Did you arrange transport from the airport to the hotel? (*please delete*)

YES / ~~NO~~ [1]

Was this service satisfactory? If not, please give brief details of any problem. [1]
No – car arrived too late

Details of rooms booked (*number and type*): [1]
<u>2 – double and family</u>

Did you eat in the hotel? (*please circle all that apply*) [1]

(BREAKFAST)   LUNCH   DINNER

SECTION C – Hotel facilities

Which facilities did you and your family use? (*please tick all that apply*)

GYM ☑   SPA ☐   POOL ☑

BUSINESS CENTRE ☑   GIFT SHOP ☐ [1]

Did the hotel arrange any tours for you? (*please delete*)   YES / ~~NO~~ [1]

If YES, which ones? (*please tick all that apply*)

PYRAMIDS ☑   COPTIC AREA ☐   EGYPTIAN MUSEUM ☑ [1]

SECTION D

In the space below, write **one** sentence of between 12 and 20 words, describing your biggest disappointment with your holiday.

(*Possible answer*) <u>I was disappointed because on two days the pool was closed and I couldn't swim.</u> (*15 words*) [2]

3 EXTENDED

Our Catania volunteer work application form

Section A – Personal details

Full name: <u>Gina Trasmundi</u> [1]

Home address: <u>via Carlotti 63, Catania, Italy</u> [1]

Email: <u>ginatras@itmail.ity</u>   Mobile/Cell number: <u>59381765</u> [1]

Section B – Education

Present school/college: <u>Catania International College (CIC)</u> [1]

What subjects are you currently studying? <u>Geography, Sociology and English as a Second Language</u> [1]

Please list **all** the previous schools you have attended, with dates.

1 <u>Catania Primary School 1999–2004</u> [1]

2 <u>Catania International Secondary School (CISS) 2004–2010</u> [1]

What qualifications do you have? (*Please tick as appropriate*)

IGCSE ☑   A Levels ☐   Other ☐ [1]

Number of passes: 6 [1]

Positions of responsibility at school/college:
Student president of school for two years 2007–2009, and secretary for the
school's environment group for one year [1]

Section C – Volunteer work

When are you available to work with Our Catania? Please circle your
preferred day and time:

Monday – Friday   (Saturday)   (Sunday)

(Mornings)   (Afternoons)   Evenings [1]

What other special skills can you offer Our Catania?

Keen artist and English language skills [1]

Section D

In the space below, write **one** sentence of between 12 and 20 words, saying
why it is important for you to join Our Catania.

(Possible answer) I'm very interested in my local environment and our water
problems and want to do something to help. *(18 words)* [2]

Exercise 4: Key

A Introduction

Check!

understand – know, comprehend

respond – answer

select – choose

organise – put things in order, arrange

recognise – be aware of

distinguish – tell things apart, know the difference

Check!

There are no big <u>differences</u> between the two papers. The text is <u>exactly</u> the same, and the task you have to complete is also <u>the same.</u> The only <u>difference</u> is that in the Core paper you need to find <u>six points</u>, whereas in the Extended paper you need to <u>find eight.</u>

B Preparation

Activity 1

Problems associated with landfill sites

Activity 2

The answers are too long and not in note form.

Activity 3

- toxic compounds entering the groundwater system
- leakage
- small risk of birth defects

Activities 4 and 5

Two answers included on one line

See answer to Activity **3**

Activities 6 and 7

Same information given twice using different words

Unpleasant smells – for other points see answer to Activity **3**

Activity 8

Does not link to the correct heading ('Problems associated with landfill sites')

Activity 9

lined waste collection points – 'Action already being taken'

deodoriser used – 'Action already being taken'

Activities 10 and 11

First answer is wrong – there is some leakage, according to the text.

population living within a two kilometre radius – is not relevant to heading

See answer to Activity **3**

Activities 12 and 13

Paragraph	Section heading	Number of points
1	none	none
2	a	1
3	b	1
4	a	2
5	none	none
6	c	3
7	c	1

Activity 14

1 (more) funds to local councils **c**

2 (unpleasant) smells **a**

3 'pay as you throw' / metered home collection system **c**

4 burying waste leads people to forget about it **a**

5   lining of collection points / protective material **b**

6   not pretty **a**

7   risk of birth defects **a**

8   tax reductions **c**

9   landfill sites are filling up **a**

10   toxic compounds entering groundwater (system) **a**

11   use of deodoriser **b**

C   Exam focus

Activity 16

Paragraph	Section heading	Number of points
1	none	none
2	a	2
3	b	4
4	none	none
5	c	2
6	none	none
7	d	1
8	d	1
9	none	none

Activity 17

Answer **3** is the best, followed by Answer **1**, and the least successful is answer **2**.

Activity 18

1 b   2 c   3 a

D **Exam practice**

1 CORE

Problems faced by clean-up group (any two details)
- poor visibility
- heavy rain destroyed roads
- transportation difficult

Rubbish collected underwater (any two details)
- plastic bottles / bags
- oil cans / pipes / shoes / ropes / rusty metal

Main causes of pollution
- lack of understanding by public
- fishermen throw rubbish into sea

2 EXTENDED

Problems with older Cairo taxis (any four details)
- run-down and falling apart
- potentially unsafe
- windows and doors that do not open and close
- heavy, thick petrol fumes
- air conditioning is unheard of

Advantages of new taxis for passengers (any four details)
- more comfortable
- only small increase in fares
- cleaner
- air conditioning on request
- functioning fare meters

3 EXTENDED

Background and development of parkour (any three details)
- evolved from obstacle course training
- original idea to return to running and jumping as basic elements
- Georges Hebert devised the training method
- term means military obstacle course

Personal and physical qualities required for parkour (any three details)
- ability to overcome obstacles
- basic skills like running, jumping and crawling

- be fit
- be neurologically coordinated
- ability to move naturally

Parkour in the gym (any two details)
- practising individual moves
- thick floor matting
- rubberised boxes

4 EXTENDED

Body's reaction to food allergies (any three details)
- swollen lips or eyes
- vomiting
- skin rashes
- difficulty breathing
- severe fall in blood pressure (anaphylactic shock)

How to diagnose food intolerance
- cut out suspected food from diet
- reintroduce food and monitor

Things to remember when cooking (any three details)
- ensure product does not contain the allergen
- store foods separately in closed containers
- wash your hands thoroughly with hot water and soap
- avoid touching other foods
- carefully wash all cooking equipment
- do not re-use oil for cooking

Exercise 5: Key

 Introduction

> **Check!**

communicate appropriately – write information in the correct way

convey information – give information

employ and control – use and manage correctly

a range of appropriate structures – different grammatical structures

observe conventions – follow the rules

> **Check!**

The main difference between the two papers is that in the Core paper, Exercise 5 <u>is linked</u> to Exercise 4. This means that you can make use of <u>the notes</u> you made in <u>Exercise 4</u> to write a 70-word summary in <u>Exercise 5</u>. For the <u>Extended paper,</u> you need to read another <u>text</u> and write a <u>summary</u> of up to 120 words from it.

Descriptors	Marks
Expression good, with attempts to group and sequence ideas in own words.	3
Expression limited **or** reliance on copying out the notes, but some sense of order.	2
Meaning obscure because of density of language errors and serious problems with expression **or** nothing of relevance.	0
Expression very good: clear, orderly grouping and sequencing, largely own words.	4
Expression weak **or** reliance on lifting from the passage.	1

B Preparation

Activity 1

1   The summary focus: describing how her behaviour has changed since her eye operation

2   Word count: about 100 words (and no more than 120 words)

3   Use own words as far as possible

Activity 2

We know that her behaviour changed after her operation.

Activity 3

Changes in her behaviour

Activity 4

Only paragraph 2 provides information for the summary.

Activity 5

All three paragraphs provide information for the summary.

Activity 6

able to reach for food – 5

can stand up for herself – 1 and 5

chased off another gorilla (Salome) who was stealing food – 2 and 5

doesn't have to feel her way around – 2

explores – 6

interacts, communicates with other gorillas – 6

now able to go outside – 6

plays with Bongo – 7

shows interest in and play-fights with a possible mate – 2 and 7

Activity 7

1   plays with Bongo **and** shows interest in, play-fights with a possible mate

2   explores **and** now able to go outside

Activity 8

Various answers possible, such as:

Sequence words	Other words
firstly, secondly, thirdly, next, then, finally, in the end, etc	however, furthermore, also, although, because, in addition, etc

Activity 9

Possible answer: Romina's behaviour has changed in several ways since her eye operation …

Activity 10

Possible answer:

Romina's behaviour has changed in several ways since her eye operation. Firstly, she is now able to chase away other gorillas when they try to steal her food, and is able to find her own food on the island. Furthermore, she is showing interest in Bongo, a possible mate, and has been seen playing with him. Also, Romina is interacting and communicating with other gorillas and standing up for herself. Finally, she no longer has to feel her way around but can see enough to go outside and explore the gorilla island, something which she could not do before her eye operation. Her life has become better in so many ways. (108 words)

C Exam focus

Activity 11

What the 'swim-with-dolphins' tourist industry should be doing to minimise the effect on dolphins

Activity 12

Students' own answers

Activity 14

Paragraphs without any relevant information: 1, 2, 4 and 6

Activity 15

Answer **1** is the best summary, followed by answer **3**, and the least successful is answer **2**.

Activity 16

1 a   2 b   3 c

Activity 17

Possible answer:

Jake Meyer has faced several mountaineering challenges during his career. Firstly, he was the youngest Briton to climb to the top of seven mountains, and achieved this in the fastest time ever. Furthermore, he keeps climbing without stopping and doesn't think about the pain he's feeling while climbing. In addition, on his latest challenge, Jake had to deal with altitude problems and several road accidents. (65 words)

Activity 18

Answer **1** is the best paragraph, followed by answer **2**, and the least successful is answer **3**.

Activity 19

1 c   2 a   3 b

D Exam practice

1 CORE

Possible answer:

The clean-up group faced several problems. Firstly, they could not see well underwater, and heavy rain had destroyed some roads. Also, transportation became difficult. When the divers went underwater, they collected plastic bags and bottles, as well as oil cans, pipes and shoes and different metals. Experts say pollution is caused by the public who do not understand the problems and by fishermen who throw rubbish into the sea. (69 words)

2 EXTENDED

Possible answer:

Jordan offers tourists a wide range of activities. Firstly, the Wadi Rum valley and desert attracts visitors who want to go on a camel safari or go trekking. Also, day visitors from Aqaba or Petra find plenty to do, such as riding Arab horses and rock-climbing. For those who wish to stay overnight, it is possible to camp under the stars. The Dead Sea is very popular with tourists for swimming and also for water spa treatments and therapies from the sea's salt and mineral content. Finally, the ancient city of Petra built into rock is an amazing attraction where tourists can look at the incredible architecture and explore life from the past. (113 words)

3 EXTENDED

Possible answer:

Nabil al Busaidi faced several problems on his journey to reach the North Magnetic Pole. To start with, the landscape and environment can change from time to time because of the movement of the ice. In addition to this, Nabil had to pull 50 kg of equipment on the 650 km journey. Also, because he was so tired, he had hallucinations which slowed him down. He also had to deal with extremely cold weather, sometimes with temperatures as low as minus 80 °C, but minus 40 °C on average. Besides the cold weather, polar bears were a problem at times, with one ripping open his tent. Finally, his relationship with his colleagues came under pressure. (112 words)

4 EXTENDED

Possible answer:

There is plenty of advice available on how to study before an exam. First of all, it is important to calm your mind as this makes studying more effective. Also, relaxing your body will help. Next, when you're studying, make sure you choose a quiet place and have all the things that you need close by. Make a list of all the important things that you need to study and then decide how much time to spend on each one. It's also important to plan your time so that you take a few minutes for breaks in between periods of studying. Finally, try to enjoy the whole experience. (108 words)

Exercises 6 and 7: Key

A Introduction

Check!

a   purpose – reason for writing (e.g. to complain about something)

format – letter, report, story, article, speech, etc.

audience – who you are writing to

b   Write *(format)* a letter to *(audience)* the magazine editor *(purpose)* telling him or her why you want to be involved.

As a member of the student council you have been asked to write *(format)* an article for your *(audience – readers of)* school magazine *(purpose)* giving your ideas about the careers day.

c   word limit, prompts, marks given

Check!

material is correct length – C

simple structures and vocabulary – L

grammatical mistakes – L

no paragraphs or paragraphs not consistent – L

some repetition of ideas – C

no understanding of the task – C

incorrect register – C

meaning is clear – L

does not quite answer the question – C

includes topics which are not relevant – C

B Preparation

Activity 1

a   letter

b   volunteer work during school holidays

c   a good friend

d informal

e style, answering the question, range of vocabulary and grammar

Activity 3

Many possibilities but safe to start with something like:

Hi John,   OR   *Dear Susan,*

How are you?   *Thanks very much for your letter.*

Activity 4

Probably 4–5: introduction, 2–3 main paragraphs, a conclusion / summing up

Activity 5

Opening 2 as it has an introduction before starting to answer the question

Activity 6

I **(a)** 've always wanted to work with children but so far I **(b)** have not had any real opportunities to do this. Both my mum and dad **(c)** are teachers and before the last summer holidays they **(d)** told me that a local youth organisation **(e)** needed volunteer workers during the holidays. I **(f)** decided that this would be an excellent opportunity for me to get some experience working with children, and so I **(g)** applied and luckily for me they **(h)** accepted my application!

Activity 7

I was really thrilled and although the work was not very difficult. I had a lot of fun.

At the start I had to arrange a programme of sports activities for the children and decide what equipment was needed for each activity.

The organisers gave me a small amount of money and it was my responsibility to go to the shops to buy all the different equipment.

And then, for the rest of the time, I helped the children with various sports. They played football, basketball, and volleyball and some of them went swimming.

Activity 8

Possible answer:

Now I have experience of working with children and I know that I enjoy it, so I would like to do it when I am older.

Take care and send me a text message soon!

John

Activity 9

a   article

b   pupils doing more to reduce waste in your school

c   readers of school magazine (students and teachers)

d   formal

e   use of persuasive language and a good, balanced argument

Activity 11

Students' own answers

Activity 13

a   3

b   4

c   1

d   2

Activity 14

Possible answer:

1   Nowadays, wastage is causing environmental problems all over the world. For example, think about the forests full of trees which are destroyed just so that we can have more books and magazines which we then simply throw away. *(38 words)*

2   Spending time thinking about the problem of wastage has several advantages. If we all put our heads together we might be able to think of ways in which we could recycle things at school. We could even think about ways to avoid using paper and other products. *(47 words)*

3   However, there may be problems for some students if they are asked to do something like this, because not everyone is interested in reducing wastage at school. Think of all those exam papers! *(33 words)*

4   Overall, this is an excellent proposal which I think everyone in our school should support. Not only will it help the environment, but it will also help to save money. *(30 words)*

(Total: 148 words)

C   Exam focus

Activity 15

Purpose – write about your new town and school

Format – a letter

Audience – a friend

Activity 16

Answer **3** is the best piece, followed by answer **2**, and the least successful is answer **1**.

Activity 17

1 c   2 a   3 b

Activity 18

Purpose – consider the advantages and disadvantages of mobile phones

Format – article for local newspaper

Audience – general public / newspaper readers

Activity 19

Answer **2** is the best piece, followed by answer **1**, and the least successful is answer **3**.

Activity 20

1 c   2 b   3 a

D   Exam practice

Students' own answers